Welcome to
MY COUNTRY

Welcome to MY COUNTRY

LAKLAK BURARRWANGA

RITJILILI GANAMBARR

MERRKIYAWUY GANAMBARR-STUBBS

BANBAPUY GANAMBARR

DJAWUNDIL MAYMURU

SARAH WRIGHT

SANDIE SUCHET-PEARSON

KATE LLOYD

ALLEN & UNWIN

SYDNEY · MELBOURNE · AUCKLAND · LONDON

First published in 2013

Allen & Unwin
83 Alexander Street
Crows Nest NSW 2065
Australia
Phone: (61 2) 8425 0100
Email: info@allenandunwin.com
Web: www.allenandunwin.com

Teachers' notes available from www.allenandunwin.com

A Cataloguing-in-Publication entry is available from the
National Library of Australia
www.trove.nla.gov.au

ISBN 978 1 74331 396 1

Cover and text design by Ruth Grüner
Set in 12 pt Minion by Ruth Grüner

Printed in China at Everbest Printing Co. Ltd

5 7 9 10 8 6 4

Australian Government

Australia | **Council**
for the Arts

This project has been assisted by the Australian Government
through the Australia Council, its arts funding and advisory body.

We belong to this land in north-east
Arnhem Land, Australia. We are Yolŋu people.
When you read this book, you'll understand who we are.
We are the first people, we were born here and we know
the language, the country, the culture.
We are Yolŋu.

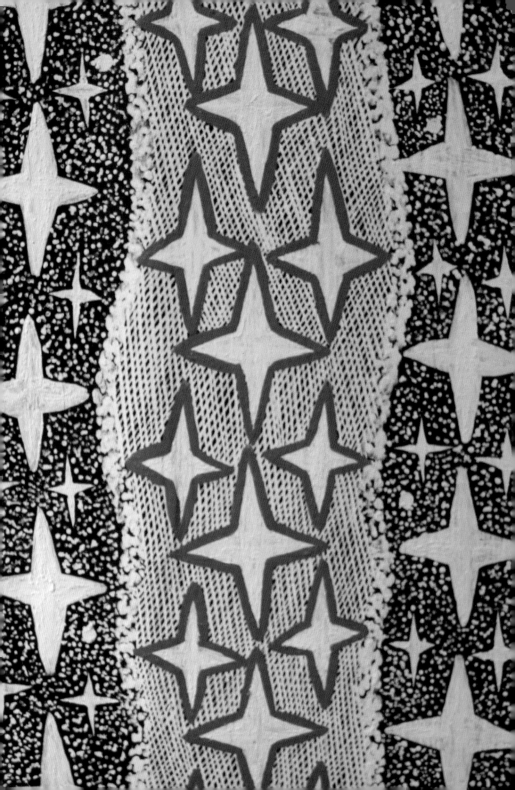

Contents

We dedicate this book to our two mums,
Gaymala Yunupiŋu and Guḻumbu Yunupiŋu:
for showing us how to go out hunting,
for giving us Yolŋu women's knowledge,
for the ideas they gave us,
for the knowledge they gave us,
for teaching us that nothing is impossible.

Raŋan, PAPERBARK

Hidden layers of Yolŋu meaning

There are eight of us bringing you this story, five sisters, two daughters and one granddaughter. Five of us are Yolŋu Indigenous people from north-east Arnhem Land; four sisters and a daughter, living at Bawaka and Yirrkala. None of us five was born in hospital. We were born on the land. That's why our babies are strong.

The other three are not Yolŋu, they are non-Indigenous women from the south of Australia who have been adopted into our family as a sister, daughter and granddaughter. We'll tell you more about that later.

Here in Bawaka, the warm sea laps the sand and we sit under tamarind, coconut and casuarina trees to keep out of the sun. We'll tell you a lot about Bawaka. It's what this book is really about, you see.

When *ŋapaki*, non-Indigenous people, come to Bawaka they see the beauty of the blue sea and the white sand,

but they don't see what *really* makes our land beautiful. They don't see the stories, the connections, the patterns, the rhythms, the songlines. In this book we want to share the true beauty of our country with you, our readers.

When *ŋapaki* come to Bawaka they wear shoes to protect their feet. But they take them off when they walk on the beach. That's when they start learning. When they're walking on the beach, they're learning the land.

To understand the Yolŋu way, you need to see everything through the *wäŋa* (homeland), through Nature and through *dhäruk* (language). *Dhäruk* is part of the Yolŋu way.

NOTE: The ŋ used in *raŋan* and *Yolŋu* and *ŋapaki* is pronounced like the 'ng' in the middle of 'singing'.

Our language allows some things to be told, it holds its own messages, its own Law.

You know how in Western societies, the rules seem to be the same wherever you go? In Yolŋu thought, to understand something properly you have to link it to one place. For us, that place is Bawaka. So as we tell you this story, we are telling it through Bawaka, our home. It is easy to learn when you learn in place. When we teach children the Yolŋu way, we take them out and show them. We walk them through. They learn the seasons, the winds, they learn how to feel and what to do. For example, when it is the season Rrarrandharr, they see how dry everything is, they feel the hot sand and learn to feel the fruits ripening. That is how we teach and how we learn. That is how we will help you learn too.

In the swamp over there, at the back of the beach, is a big *raŋan*, a paperbark tree. If you go closer, you'll see the bark; this peels away and below it is more bark. It is all intertwined. That's our Yolŋu knowledge – there are layers and layers of it, stored in old people's heads. And we're making new knowledge too, all the time, making new songs.

So come and spend some time with us at Bawaka. Spend some days, and some nights, getting a taste of what Bawaka is like at different times of the year, during different seasons, hearing some stories and learning about how things connect in our Yolŋu world. The songlines at Bawaka all end at *djäpana*, sunset. Our songlines are like a map, they show where everything goes. So, here, at the end of each of our days at Bawaka, we will end with *djäpana* too.

So come on, let us begin.

yothu-yindi gapu manbuyŋa

1

Gapu, WATER

A system for everything

Can you see that *gapu,* that water, there? It is so calm that when the moon goes past you can see its reflection like the inside of your heart. That is what it is like at this time of year, the season we know as Dharraddharradya. It usually starts in June or July, but the exact date (in the Western calendar) shifts slightly each year. The beginning of a season comes with a wind or a flower or the appearance of an animal or a feeling. The land tells us when there is a new season, not the calendar.

If you come to Bawaka from the south during Dharraddharradya, you will be escaping the cold winter. Here we can still sleep outside, but it's cool at night so we'll make a fire.

If there aren't any blankets around we'll use some *raŋan*, paperbark, for making a bed. Thick layers of *raŋan* will keep us warm. There usually isn't any rain at this time of year and there aren't any mosquitoes.

It's a beautiful time to visit Bawaka. The water is calm. Before we fall asleep, maybe a few clouds will drift across the sky. We can always see all the stars at this time of year. You can also see the moonlight going along its own path across the land, touching the water, touching your heart.

Yirritja and Dhuwa, *yothu* and *yindi*

Now we will sit here, under the *djomala* (casuarina trees) and look at the *gapu*, the water. The more you look, the more you see. Can you tell that there is more than one water there? When we Yolŋu look, we see two *gapu*. The top one is Yirritja, and comes from Yirritja country. Bawaka is Yirritja country. The bottom *gapu* is Dhuwa and comes from Dhuwa country next to us. The *gapu* is connected to us Yolŋu people, because we are also always Dhuwa and Yirritja. Everything in our world is either one or the other. It's a bit like yin and yang in an Eastern way of thinking.

Yirritja and Dhuwa tell us how everything is connected and how things are woven together. The child of a Yirritja mother, for example, is Dhuwa. The husband of a Dhuwa woman is Yirritja. Our land at Bawaka is Yirritja. The land next to it is Dhuwa. Yirritja and Dhuwa, Dhuwa and Yirritja, they give rise to each other in turn. Together they make a whole.

As Bawaka is Yirritja, and I (Laklak) and my sisters are mothers of that land, we must be Dhuwa. Do you see? That land next to Bawaka is its mother too. It's Dhuwa land. So Bawaka has its mother there right beside it, the land called Yalangbara, and it has its mothers, me and my sisters, living on it. All of us have a special responsibility to take care of that place. There are a lot of mothers, a lot of children, a lot of aunties and uncles and kin in the Yolŋu world.

This relationship between mother and child is very, very important to Yolŋu. It exists between people, and between people and the land. This mother–child relationship is what we call *yothu-yindi*. Perhaps you have heard of the famous Yolŋu band, Yothu-Yindi. Now you know what the name means. The *yindi* is the mother, *yothu* is the child. A *yothu-yindi* relationship can be between two people or between two pieces of land like Bawaka and Yalangbara across the water. One is always Dhuwa and one Yirritja. Yirritja can be the mother for Dhuwa, or Dhuwa can be the mother for Yirritja. It is a web that weaves and holds everyone and everything together. Through Yirritja

3

and Dhuwa, what anthropologists call 'moieties', everything is interconnected and interdependent.

It is not just people that have a moiety; trees, animals, rocks and soil, winds, spirits, ancestors, clouds, stories and songs are either Yirritja or Dhuwa also. We are connected as kin to animals and plants and to things that aren't even considered living in other cultures. The word *djäpana* (sunset) is a Yirritja word – we'll tell you the Dhuwa word for sunset later.

See that rock over there, that rock might be Dhuwa. If you are Dhuwa too, perhaps that rock is your sister or your father. As a Dhuwa person, you would have a song about that rock as you have songs about Dhuwa things, Dhuwa land, Dhuwa people. Yirritja people sing about Yirritja things, Yirritja land, Yirritja rocks, Yirritja winds, Yirritja animals, everything Yirritja. Yirritja people sing songs about this land Bawaka, about people sitting in the shade of the *djomala*, just as we are doing now.

So when we say there is Yirritja and Dhuwa water, we mean that the two *gapu* come from different places, that they complement each other, that together they make up a whole. It is as if the whole world is contained in that relationship, one that holds and brings everything together. It is breathing, it is everyday life, it is every part of the body and how it works. It works through the land, language, dance, song.

That's enough talking for the moment. Let's go collect some *maypal*, some oysters.

Feast on the rocks

During Dharraddharradya, when it is cool and dry, the *maypal* are so creamy and good. They've got a lot of juice in them. We'll walk to where there is a good rock with plenty of *maypal*. You go grab the chisel, we'll use that to get them off the rock. Djawundil will get some water – we always keep some in the freezer so it will be nice and cool to drink after a hot walk. We'll bring the kids along. They can play at the edge of the water while we work. Roger the dog can follow along too. Then we'll talk more as we eat the *maypal* around the fire with a cup of tea. Later, when we get back to the house, we'll have the smoking ceremony to welcome you properly to Country.

To get those *maypal* we're going to head towards the Dhuwa land next to Bawaka. For us, the land is not one big mass but is made up of different *wäŋa*, different homelands. These are like patchwork as they go from Dhuwa to Yirritja and Yirritja to Dhuwa in that *yothu-yindi*, or mother–child relationship we spoke of. The land is rich with meaning and there are signs and stories everywhere. You can go anywhere and see a river, tree, hill or rock telling us a story that this is a Dhuwa place or a Yirritja place.

We learn the knowledge from our grandparents, walking in the land, telling the stories. Or we sing the songlines. Like that hill over there – we know it is Dhuwa country. We are connected to the landscape, the land is family, we are related to the land, and everything tells us a story. If we are Yirritja we can go hunting on Dhuwa land, but we will ask permission, and if we are successful we take the owners some of our catch. That's the Law.

Tourists and *ŋapaki* must learn about the land, whether it is Dhuwa or Yirritja. They also need to know if it's a sacred area. They should go with a tour guide who will tell them what is okay to photograph and what is not. There was a problem once when a lady took a photo of an island that is very important to us. You're not allowed to take photos in a sacred area. We told her to delete the photo.

Here, take a piece of *dhalimbu*, of hard shell, to prise the oysters off the rock. We'll talk as we chip away at the oysters. Thunk, thunk, chip, chip, tap. You have to get it in just the right place so the *dhalimbu* doesn't slide off but breaks the oyster open instead. Not too soft, not too hard. That's right. It's good, gathering oysters. A good time to laugh and talk and to eat some as we go. They are so slippery, juicy and salty. Good eating.

That's enough *maypal* now. We will leave plenty for the future. Here we have a good amount for a feed. Djawundil has started a fire. Let's join her with these *maypal*. We can eat and have a cup of tea. Look around as we go. Notice the grass is all dry. It's ready to be burnt to clear up the old grass and get ready for Nature to grow, to have fresh food. Drink some tea and listen.

Can you see that *gapu*, that water, there near the rocks? It is Dhuwa and Yirritja *gapu*. It's all tangled up, like the different colours in a pile of pandanus ready for weaving. When the water is deeper, we call it the Yirritja word *manbuyŋa* (deep ocean water). Where the rivers run rough

coming into the calm water, we call it the Yirritja words *betj* or *mungulk*. When the Yirritja waters are calm, we call them *naykuna* or *marrawuluḻ*. We have Dhuwa words for Dhuwa *gapu* too: *ritjilili*, my sister's name, means waves, *mutitj* means peaceful *gapu*.

We don't get our knowledge from a calendar or a book, we just know, and it's been that way for thousands and thousands of years, from when the old people were still alive, forever. The old people knew the mix of fresh water and salt water. Women and men and children now, we know what's rough, calm, heavy, light; what's floating or not floating; where the *gapu* is salty, where it's fresh. We know what to look for, we know what the distance, the weight, the height, the colour means. Of course we make mistakes sometimes.

Smoking you welcome

It's time now to welcome you properly to Bawaka. We'll have a smoking ceremony. You stand over here; you can see the *gapu*, the water, from here. We need to be under the shade and off that hot sand. We've collected some leaves of the *djilka* tree for the ceremony. Here, we put them on the fire until they start to smoke. Now we brush them over you to welcome you here. Close your eyes and breathe deep. Smell that cleansing smoke. We will ask Bayini, a spirit of Bawaka, to protect and care for you: '*Golulu dhipala wä alili arrakala Bawakalili.*' 'We are welcoming you to this place of Bawaka.'

When *ŋapaki* come to Bawaka for the first time we always have a smoking ceremony. Welcome ceremonies are very important to Yolŋu people. *Djilka* is a special tree that we use for the cleansing ceremony. It gets the spirit out, takes it away and replaces it with Bawaka spirit, so the land and the sea and Bayini will recognise you and will look after you. Bayini is a beautiful young woman who protects us here. She has millions of eyes to see everything you do. She will see bad or good things. Bayini protects the people and the land.

Bayini was a *Mangatharra* (Macassan) who came to us from Indonesia long ago. In my grandfather's time, and long before that too, Mangatharra used to travel down from their place up north in Indonesia to Arnhem Land to trade. They used to come at the beginning of the wet season with the north-west wind. They came in Macassan boats called *prahu*s. The Aboriginal people traded trepang, sea cucumber, and the Mangatharra traded knives and material. They also introduced smoking – you know, with a pipe – and rice. They taught the Yolŋu how to make pottery and they planted tamarind trees.

We have a story about Bayini and how she came to Bawaka.

One time they anchored in the mouth of the bay and there was a lady on the boat called Bayini. She was a beautiful lady and a princess but she was a slave on the boat. She had to work, cooking and making clothes for the boss, the leader of the Mangatharra. Then she saw land, and she rose up and took the sword from the captain. She had pride because she was a princess and she got the sword. They threw her into the sea and she swam all the way to the other side of the bay. She's got a footprint in the rock there. You can see it.

Bayini slept on the rock, drying herself. Then when she woke up she named places like Bungulu, where she landed, which we also call Bayini Beach. She had long hair to her thighs, and wore gold rings and necklaces. She walked straight to Bawaka. There's the area with the tamarind tree. That's where she cooked rice. She had a shelter there too, and maybe a husband. After she died she remained, protecting Bawaka.

When you're out at the point you can see a sandbar that ends in a rock under the water and that's an anchor from the boat she came on. There's a chain that runs all the way to the edge of our land. You can see the rock she slept on too.

Her spirit is still living and protecting the land here and on the other side. We are asking her to protect you with this welcome ceremony. She will take care of you as long as you behave well and care for the land and Nature. Don't forget she has millions of eyes.

Do you smell that smoke? Feel it cleansing you. The land will recognise you now and look after you. You will be protected from the snake, the spider and from other kinds of harm. Don't forget, Bayini is always here.

The land and the spirits, the sea and all the beings are respected in a Yolŋu world. The sea there, it has its own *wäŋa*, its own system and patterns of behaviour. The *guya* (fish), the *maranydjalk* (stingray), and the *miyapunu* (turtle), have each got their own language. That's why male and female turtles, when they meet, they know each other, they can talk. They've got their special home under the sea – Yirritja and Dhuwa. All the different animals, they have their own groups. Seagulls, crows, they live by themselves, they have their own rules, style of talking and living with one another, their own language. The birds and animals know where to sleep, where to put their babies, where to build their nests. The same for trees, bushes. The land knows what their language is.

Hear that? The wind in the trees by the beach? They whisper, they sing, they whistle. These are my favourite trees, here by my house on the beach. They make me sleep. And this is all connected to people. When *bäru*, the crocodile, dies, my mother cries, because she is related to *bäru*. This all goes through the songline. Yolŋu sing and pretend they're the birds. Yolŋu can sing the bush turkey, the seagulls.

Every tree, water, rock, has a language. You hear the water? 'Wa.' There, do you hear it? That's the water talking, the sound of the water rushing on to the sand. We understand the tides, the way the water moves and changes. We hear the language as we sit on the land. Also through ceremony and through song.

'Wa.' That's in the song. It's the language of water. Even when you walk through the sand you can hear the sand talk to you. That's the language of sand. The land knows.

So here we are at *djäpana*, the sunset. Look at those lovely rich colours. There are pinks, reds and oranges. The way the clouds lie across the sky is like the strands of a beautiful woven basket.

We're going to tell you a story to end this day. It's just coming into *guku* season, honey season, so Merrki is going to tell you a story about honey. It's a good story to end a day during Dharraddharradya. The story also tells you about the *gapu*, the water. It's about Barrkira, to the west of here. We have family there.

The Honey-water story

MERRKI: This story is a Dhuwa story. It is the story of the *Guku-Gapu*, the Honey-water. It is about the body of water at a place called Barrkira, an ancient tree, Guymululu, and three ancestral beings: Mayawa, the frill-necked lizard, and two spirit beings, Wulugarrk and Birrinydjalpi. Listen now.

Guymululu was a massive, ancient tree that stood between Barrkira and a place called Rirramul. Mayawa, the frill-necked lizard saw honey in that big old tree and began to gorge itself. Mayawa greedily ate as much of that honey as possible until a sharp splinter made it choke.

'What is it, friend?' called the other spirits, Wulugarrk and Birrinydjalpi.

'It's choking me! Choking me, friends!' he replied and ran straight up a tree.

'Quick, give us the dillybag,' said the other two. Hearing this, Mayawa threw the bag down.

The two spirit beings filled the tightly woven bag to the brim with wild honey. They lifted the bag up to their shoulders but it burst, spilling the honey everywhere! It flowed from that bag into the waters nearby, and it kept flowing out, out into the ocean. And there it is where the current still runs. Today it still empties itself into the waters of Yilipa.

The honey kept flowing and turned into two massive currents, and these two currents spoke to each other, still calling each other friends. They came upon the place of a creature spirit, the shark, but she was sleeping and they decided to let her be. And they kept going out, out into the deepest sea. There the Honey-water clashed with other Yirritja and Dhuwa waters.

'Let us stop here, my friend,' said one spirit. 'We shall rest here forever, in this place we shall call Yilipa.'

It was the honey that flowed out there; now it is just water.

The spiral in a woven basket shows
the life cycle – tells us how babies grow,
their arteries and their selves, both in the
womb and as growing children and on through
the generations. As the basket grows, so a baby
girl grows up until she's a young mother and
she'll learn and have babies, and the knowledge
and growth keeps spiralling. The woman becomes
a grandmother and the cycle keeps going.
There's no actual death, life keeps spiralling
on through the generations

LAKLAK BURARRWANGA

Laklak's Story 1

WALKING AND RAFTING ACROSS ARNHEM LAND

Hello, my name is Laklak. I am an elder for the Datiwuy people (my father's clan) and a caretaker for the Gumatj clan (my mother's) in north-east Arnhem Land. These are two of the thirteen clans that make up the Yolŋu-speaking people.

I am the eldest sister and the eldest child in our family. That means I have a special responsibility to care for the family, to care for the country, and to help educate people. For me, that means helping ŋapaki, non-Indigenous people, understand about Yolŋu. I will tell you my story because it says a lot about my people's history and wishes for the future.

Arnhem Land is in the tropical far north of Australia. It's a big place, a place that has always belonged to us Yolŋu and that we belong to as well. It is full of story, ceremony and sacred places.

Before I was born, my mother and father went hunting and they found many, many *warrapal* (cockles). The shells are usually just plain white but these were colourful! An old lady said to Mum and Dad, *'Dhika yothu bay!'* ('Maybe someone will have a baby!') She explained that even though I wasn't born yet, I had brought those cockles for my parents. Later she had a dream about me.

My father, he had other wives and many other children. He didn't live with us, but would just come and visit. When I was six, Mum thought it was time to leave that place, Rorrowuy, and go to Yirrkala, where the mission was, and where she had family. She was thinking about education. Mum wanted us to learn the ŋapaki (whitefella) way too, so that we could live life in both worlds. So we had to walk a very long way across Arnhem Land to get to Yirrkala. (You can see from the map, pages 198–9.)

I tell you, it is a very long way to walk! There were six of us kids: Djali, Merrki, Ritjilili, Garyarr, Guluwu and me. Mum was pregnant too. Even though I was only six, I sometimes had to carry my little sisters Merrki and Ritjilili.

I still remember that walk. It took fifteen hours. Mum protected us from buffalo and dingo. She helped us across creeks and found us fruit and yams to eat. It was very hot. This was during Rrarranhdharr, that's a hot season for walking, but Mum knew where to find waterholes. We didn't take much, just some dilly-bags with clothes, and some tools. We carried duṯtji (firesticks) with us to light fires – you hold coals in a pandanus trunk and it burns forever.

We came to a big stretch of water, a big river. We stopped and cut some small trees and lashed them together with raŋan (paper-bark) to make a raft. We put the little kids on the raft and then I got on. We were drifting out to the middle of the river, with Mum still on the bank.

When we were halfway across, a pigeon called out, 'Gooooo goooook, gooooo goooook.' That pigeon was telling us there were sharks nearby! It was the change of tide, and the pigeon was telling the people, and the sharks too, that it was time for the sharks to go upriver. The birds were giving us messages and talking to each other.

Mum was on the other bank, crying out, 'What am I going to do?' I decided I had to swim. I jumped out and pushed the raft the rest of the way, safely across to the other side. Mum

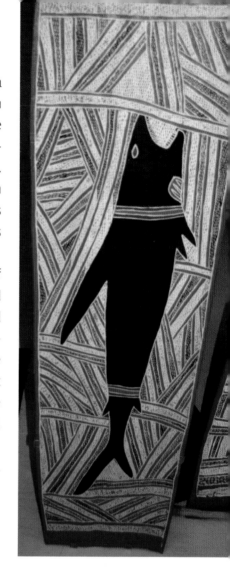

thought, 'Well, I can't leave them there by themselves, sharks or no sharks, crocodile or anything, I'll just swim across.' Mum was heavily pregnant but she swam across too and guided us safely on to Yangunbi.

When we got to Yangunbi, on Melville Bay, Mum lit a fire for her dad to see. When Granddad saw the fire he knew we were coming, so he sailed in his *lipalipa* (dugout canoe) to meet us. His *lipalipa* was called Gurtha (Fire) and he brought us all across the bay in it.

Grandma and Granddad were staying at that place with their other children, including all my mum's other sisters and all their grandchildren. They were sitting on the beach when we got there. They rushed over, throwing themselves on the ground they were so happy to see us.

My grandma especially was so happy, so emotional, she was wailing and throwing herself on the ground. We ran to her and hugged her and all these other women started wailing as well. You know, it's a kind of welcome. And of course Mum was doing the same thing.

This is where I met all the family, all my relations I didn't know. They kept saying, 'I'm your cousin, your uncle (or whatever)'. People like Mandawuy – you know Mandawuy Yunupiŋu from the band Yothu Yindi? – were there; they were just young kids then. It was very confusing, to meet such a lot of people at once.

We had made it safely all the way across Arnhem Land, through the bush, through that river, across the bay, and afterwards we made it to Yirrkala, the mission town. That was the beginning of the journey that brought me to my homeland of Bawaka.

Later on I'll tell you more about my life, about the journey that I took to get from Yirrkala to this place. I will tell you about the land-rights movement, the homelands movement, the push for schooling in Indigenous languages, and our family's place in all that. And I'll tell you about our homeland of Bawaka and what it means to us.

NOTE: Laklak's story has been developed through many conversations over the years. This account builds on the work done by Dr Sophie Creighton, who recorded, transcribed and edited it together with Laklak and her sisters and their late mother's sister, Gulumbu Yunupiŋu.

2

Miyapunu, TURTLE

Counting and sharing

Little showers of rain come through Bawaka now. It's still Dharraddharradya season, but now it's August. They are lovely, these showers. On a hot day they really cool you down. These rains make the land and sea beautiful. It's good to go fishing after this rain. And yes, it's good to go and get *miyapunu*, turtle, and *miyapunu mapu*, turtle eggs.

Today we're going to talk a bit about counting and sharing. Sharing is one of the most important things for Yolŋu. We're going to take you out to collect some *miyapunu mapu*. You'll see how we count them and divide them up. We're going to cook and divide up that *miyapunu* too.

The importance of sharing, and the responsibility to share, is called *wetj*. Sharing is so important to Yolŋu that there are a lot of stories about it. Some of them talk about what can happen if you *don't* share. They're like a warning and a teaching at the same time. At the end of our day together, we'll tell you one of those stories. It's about Djet, the sea eagle.

A ride in the troopies

We get *miyapunu mapu* from Lilirrtja, the long beach. There is a big mob of us, so let's go in the troopies, the troop carriers. We'll all pile into the two of them. You can fit a lot of people, *bukmak*, in the back on those sideways seats. Hold on tight.

On the way we'll see all the grass that's been knocked down by *dhimurru* winds. In Dharraddharradya season the grass is really dry, it's dying and ready for burning. The leaves are falling down too. It's windy, the winds this time of year make the waves go bigger and help to push the *miyapunu* in to the beach. The nights are cool, so we like to sit next to the fire to keep warm. And look, over to the right is the point. You can peer over the edge and see fish, dolphins, even dugong sometimes, far below in the clear water.

If you asked one of us, 'How many people are going along on this trip to gather *miyapunu mapu*?', that person would reply, 'As well as you, there are the sisters, Laklak, Ritjilili, Banbapuy and Merrki, plus their daughter Djawundil, granddaughter Nanukala, great-granddaughter/ mother Mawunymula (Shyrell), and great-grandson/uncle Garranhthalu. And there is the other sister Ralapiny (Sandie) and Sandie's children Raṉi, Lalu and Gara; plus daughter Ruwuk (Kate) and her children, Miyapunu and Galpu; and then a granddaughter of Laklak and her sisters through the paternal line, Madirriny (Sarah), and her daughter Dawu, who is auntie to Laklak and her sisters.' Yes, that's right, Dawu is my auntie and Mawunymula my mother even though they are a toddler and a little girl. We'll explain that more when we talk kinship and connection later on.

All up, you might have been expecting a simple answer like, 'There are eighteen of us in our group.' What we answered, though, is the Yolŋu way and is really a better answer. For us, kinship lies at the heart of everything. A world with no kinship is a world that does not have a true existence. Kinship gives everything meaning, order, balance.

Now, here we are at the edge of the beach. We'll just walk down this slope and be out on the sand. It's a great long stretch of sand all the way from Lilirrtja to Yalangbara and open to the sea. This is a very significant beach because this is where the Djan'kawu, two sisters, the creators of our

25

world, came ashore in their canoe. That makes this beach the centre of things. It's a very special place.

Here, as we walk along, we see the water running over the sand. That is where the sisters landed and started off on their sacred journey. All of our history is here in the land.

As we walk, we are looking for the tracks of the mother *miyapunu* on the sand.

The *miyapunu* are special animals to us. We have gathered their *mapu* in this way for as long as this world has existed. We make sure that we don't take too much. We respect those *miyapunu* and we see that their well-being and our well-being are connected. That is part of the great pattern of kinship that we have been talking about. We sustain them, and they sustain us. We also sing their songs, dance and cry. The most significant for us, the one with the songline, is *dhalatpu*, the green turtle.

One way that we respect the *miyapunu* is to hunt them at the proper time. For us, the proper time to hunt *miyapunu* and also to gather the eggs is during Dharraddharradya. It is nice and cool at this time of year. There might be a fog on the beach and the sand is really cold under our feet. It is the season for *miyapunu* to come and lay her eggs. *Gaypal*, the wattle, is flowering now. The *gaypal* is a messenger that tells us the time is right to hunt *miyapunu*. The mud crabs have a lot of meat on them too, the snakes are laying their eggs and the *guya*, fish, are fat. That is what the *gaypal* tells us when we see its masses of yellow flowers. It is like that for all animals, all food-gathering. There is a time, a season, that is right. There are connections there between plants and animals and people, there are patterns that underlie our universe.

Seeing the different flowers tells us a lot. The yellow of the *gaypal* tells the cold to come up, so it's windy. That will bring the *miyapunu*. The message from the *gaypal* is that we feel the flowering and in our heart, our soul, we feel the future. Before the flower opens, we feel the season will be coming: we anticipate the season unfolding. We're hoping, wishing, 'Come on, *miyapunu*, when is the flowering?', because we feel it is time and we want to eat. When it happens, the size of the flower shows us something too. The big flower is good.

'Look!' cries Mawunymula. She points to where a *miyapunu* has been. We can see the track going up and coming down and we know a *miyapunu* has laid her eggs there. Let us gather some eggs. We will take them back to the camp to share. We get a stick and put it in the sand. We feel where it is soft and where it is hard. Doing this we go around and find where the turtle eggs are, how deep the eggs are. When it is soft, that is where there are eggs. It is hard work digging up the eggs. Those eggs can be buried deep. We will take turns digging while the children play on the sand. There are a lot here, we'll have a lot to share when we return to camp.

Today the men have gone hunting for *miyapunu* as well, in a boat. Djawa, my eldest son, is taking them. Around this time of year, the *miyapunu* move away from eating in the bays like those around Bawaka and go out into the ocean to breed. When the men go hunting they can see the *miyapunu* mating. Then the male goes back to the rivers and into the bay to eat more, and the female comes up on shore to lay her *mapu*. That is what is happening at this time of year, so we know there will be eggs for us to find. Maybe the men will be successful and we can show you not only how to count and share the eggs but also how to prepare and share the *miyapunu*.

Now we have our *miyapunu mapu* we all pile in to the troopie and drive back to the house. We're hot and dusty and the kids are looking forward to a swim. Here, have some cool water.

Back at the house, we just have time to boil the kettle for tea before the men arrive back in the boat from their hunt.

Back from the hunt

Some boys went with the men to watch them hunt. They call out excitedly from the boat, '*Miyapunu!*' They do sign language with their hands on their necks, making a slitting motion.

We sign back, *Nhämunha*'? (How many?) with the hand flipped over. Then, using our fingers we sign, 'Do you have *waŋgany* or *marrma* – one or two?'

They sign back *waŋgany*. Djawa and the men have caught *waŋgany miyapunu*, one turtle. The boys are waving and we can see the smiles on their faces. Hunting *miyapunu* from a small boat with a spear is difficult and dangerous. It is very exciting when there is a successful hunt.

The men come splashing through the shallows, carrying

the *miyapunu,* which is still alive, to where we sit around the fire. It is time for some tea so we build up the fire to cook the turtle meat. Everyone is happy and excited. We have *miyapunu* and *miyapunu mapu.* It is a big occasion!

First, we prepare the *miyapunu* for cooking. Djawa kills the *miyapunu.* He hits it over the head with a rock or an axe to stun it. Then he puts a sharp stick into the head, through the brain, to kill it. He cuts its head off and then pulls the guts out through its neck. He draws out the liver, the intestines, all sweet and fatty. This female *miyapunu* has *mapu* in her, soft ones, and we pull them out to cook. We don't have a pot here so we will cook the *mapu* on the sand by covering them with ashes. We have built up a big fire for the *miyapunu,* so there is a lot of hot sand we can use to cook the *mapu.*

We dig through the hot sand and bury the *mapu* taken from inside the *miyapunu* together with the *mapu* collected on the beach. Maybe ten minutes later they're ready. The *mapu* are salty and rich. They taste like the sea. We might also eat the first lot of the *miyapunu,* the inside parts, at the same time. Nothing is wasted. That's respect.

To start cooking the *miyapunu,* we put stones in the fire to heat them up. We stand the *miyapunu* up on its back legs and put the hot stones inside the shell with some *djilka* leaves, the ones used for the smoking ceremony, as herbs. The *djilka* have got a really good smell. They'll make the meat good and tasty. You put those leaves in with the hot stones and wait for half an hour or so. We get a soup from that mixture, a salty, fragrant broth that comes from the inside of the shell where the meat has been soaked through with the herbs. We'll all take a drink of that soup – old people, young people, all of us. It's good. It makes you feel strong and alive.

Now we put the *miyapunu* in the fire to cook. We put some ashes on the top too and wait about an hour until it is ready. It's softer to cut now. We cool it down with sea water.

Cut and share

It is really important that *miyapunu* and *miyapunu mapu* are cut up, divided and shared properly. This is Yolŋu custom; we know how to cut the animal up and how to share it out through singing and dancing. The new generations all learn this way to cut and share.

The way that we share food tells a lot about relationships. It tells us about kin, about respect and duty, about who is close and who is distant. Sometimes we share to make those who are far away come close. It is important to our identity as Yolŋu.

When we cut up any animal we've hunted – *djunuŋ-guyaŋu* (dugong), *garrtjambal* (red kangaroo), *dhum'thum* (wallaby), and *miyapunu* – all the different pieces of the animal have names. There is a special way of cutting up the animal and a special way of distributing it. So, for example, the tail of *garrtjambal* goes to the people that went with the hunter. No one misses out. It's the same whenever the men go hunting, whenever the women get *ganguri*, yam.

Everything is shared, the meat, the *miyapunu mapu*, even the shopping!

The first lot of our *miyapunu* we share with family, with children. That's the soft eggs from inside the body and the *ruwu*, the guts. Everybody gets some of the inside. The next part is for the people who went hunting. Everyone on the boat has roles. Perhaps they drove the boat or acted as a spotter or assisted the hunter. The special skill of carving the meat means there are special cuts of the meat for each of them.

Afterwards the men cut the rest of the meat into different parts. When the meat is finished, when all that is left is the shell of the *miyapunu*, they give out the meat. The women are there close by to receive and distribute it. Each family gets some – one family, and then the next, until it's finished. No one misses out, and if there is a lot left we send it to other people, like our family on the other side of the bay at Dhaniya, or we take it to Yirrkala and share it with families there.

Dividing up food from a hunt like this one is an important kind of sharing, but we Yolŋu have sharing patterns for all kinds of things in life – for *rupiyah*, money, or food bought from the store, or anything. We use these kinds of exchanges to look after each other and be true to our relationships. The way we divide, distribute and share food is done carefully depending on the food and who is involved. At different times it is the responsibility of men, women, even children.

While that meat is cooking, let's divide up the eggs. We can use it to teach you about our numbering system.

Eggs and numbers

When we collect *miyapunu mapu* we get *dhaŋaŋ* (lots and lots) of *mapu*. Sometimes there are 80 or more in just one nest. Sometimes we might find a few nests along the beach so we have many, many *mapu*. There's a special way of counting them and sharing them with the family.

First, we put all the eggs in groups of five. We do it carefully, putting four eggs together on the sand and one on top. That little pile of eggs we call one *rulu*. Let's do that now with all these eggs that we have. Remember, put four in a square and the fifth goes on top, like a little pyramid. We'll spread them out here on the sand under the tree.

Rulu is a word for that pile of five eggs. The *rulu* is the basis of Yolŋu numbering (rather than ten, as in the decimal system). Although it comes from our dividing up of *miyapunu mapu*, we use this same system to count a set or group of anything.

So, to count from one to four, we go: *waŋgany* (one), *marrma* (two), *lurrkun* (three), *dämbu miriw* (four). Five is one set, so it is *waŋgany rulu* (one set).

To get to six, you take one set of five and add one: *Waŋgany rulu ga waŋgany* (*ga* means 'and'). In English, that means one set and one extra. Or you could translate it as five plus one which equals six. To get, say, fifteen you need three sets of five or *lurrkun rulu*. Twenty is four sets of five: *dämbu miriw* (four) *rulu* (lots of five).

1	*waŋgany*
2	*marrma*
3	*lurrkun*
4	*dämbu miriw*
5	*waŋgany rulu*
6	*waŋgany rulu ga waŋgany*
7	*waŋgany rulu ga marrma*
8	*waŋgany rulu ga lurrkun*
9	*waŋgany rulu ga dämbu miriw*
10	*marrma rulu*
15	*lurrkun rulu*
20	*dämbu miriw rulu*
22	*dämbu miriw rulu ga marrma baythinyawuy* (*baythinyawuy* = more)

When we say *rulu*, we usually mean a set of five but if the context is clear, it could be used to mean any other set. If we have one row of, say, 20 and another row of 20, then you could say *marrma rulu* for the two sets of 20. So that's a short way to say 40. The full way is longer and is used when the context is not clear. In that case, 40 would be two sets of 20 with the 20 spelt out as four sets of five. That would give us *marrma* (two lots of) *dämbu miriw* (four) *rulu* (lots of five) or, to leave out the English, *marrma dämbu miriw rulu*.

There is another word that we use for counting, *mala*. *Mala* means 'clan' and it also means 'ten'. In the Yolŋu way, our counting is abstract but it is also based in real things like *miyapunu mapu* and families or clans. So, if we are here at Bawaka and we call someone in Yirrkala to ask them to come out to see us, we might say, 'Let's be *waŋgany mala*. Let's be one clan.'

Let's look at how you can use *mala* as 'ten'. So, to give you a puzzle, 'What is *waŋgany rulu ga waŋgany rulu*?' Can you figure it out? First, let's translate the question. We asked, 'What is one set of five plus one set of five?' (Did you get that? *Ma*, good.) Now, there are two ways of answering the question. The more common way would be, 'That is *marrma rulu*. That is two sets of five.' Another way, using *mala*, would be to answer, 'That is *waŋgany mala*, that is one lot of ten.' It would be unusual but it would still be right.

To get back to our *mapu* on the beach, there are a lot of people here today. Country has shared with us and so we share among ourselves. So, we say 'Djawundil, you can have *lurrkun rulu*.' Djawundil will come and get her fifteen

35

eggs. 'Lirrina can have *marrma rulu*.' That's ten for her. And so on. Lirrina might eat some there and put the rest in a container to take home with her to Yirrkala.

The little babies and kids don't get any *rulu*. They just get *waŋgany* or *marrma mapu*, one or two eggs. There are different amounts for different families and we give bigger families more eggs. A family with two children might get *marrma rulu*, two of the sets of five. If there are any left over we might give one or two eggs direct to the children.

A Yolŋu maths test!

Let's see if you followed along.

In Yolŋu counting how do you write these?

2   8   24

If we call out to Dhangdhang, 'You can have *waŋgany rulu*,' how many eggs does she get?

If Banbapuy gets *marrma rulu ga marrma*, how many is that?

If we had a total of *marrma dämbu miriw rulu ga marrma* eggs, how many did we gather?

Marrma (two) lots of *ḏämbu miriw rulu* (20) *ga* (and) *marrma* (two) gives 42 eggs
Banbapuy gets 12 eggs
Dhangdhang will get 5 eggs
24 = *ḏämbu miriw rulu* (four lots of five) *ga ḏämbu baythinyawuy* (and four more)
8 = *waŋgany rulu ga lurrkun*
2 = *marrma*

Sharing and respect

The counting that we talked about here may seem similar to Western mathematics. But for us the knowledge of when to hunt, the way of describing who is along with us and the ethic of sharing are all really mathematics too. It is all about patterns. For us mathematics is not just about counting. Yolŋu mathematics is the natural way. It is in the land.

So now let's rest in the shade a little. It has been a big day. It's a beautiful thing to do, to share food that you have hunted, to cook it well and to share it properly with your friends and loved ones. And we do it in a way that respects the *miyapunu* too, that respects the land. It is all about sharing.

It is important to share because it the Law. It is the system from the old people, going back thousands and thousands of years, for ever. This system has been standing really strong. So our mob, we grow up, and we see those rules. We have been told, 'You must not be greedy. You have to share with everyone.'

We have been told, and we have the knowledge in our heads, what we have to share with the family. It is a cycle of sharing. You share with some, others share with you. It doesn't matter if you're in the city or wherever, we always share. That's *wetj*: sharing and responsibility.

Now it is nearly *djäpana*, sunset, so we'll tell you another story to end our day while we sit here next to the warm fire waiting for that *miyapunu* to be done. It's nice and cool now in the early evening. The light is just changing colour and soon there will be a lovely sunset. We'll tell you a story about the importance of sharing.

The story of Djet, the sea eagle

This story is about a father and his son Djet. One day Djet, his father, his mother, his grandfather and grandmothers and sister went fishing. They walked up the beach, walking and walking, going to where the big shade was. They put down all their gear under the shade and made a fire. Djet's *ŋändi* (mother), *yapa* (sister), *märi* (mother's mother) and *momo* (father's mother) said, 'You stay here, we are going to get *ganguri*, yams.'

So the women went off to gather yams and left the men to fish.

The little boy Djet said to his father, 'Father, I want to go and get some sand crabs for you to use as bait.'

He walked along the beach looking for sand crabs. He suddenly saw a white fish in the water.

'Wei!' he called. 'What is that? I'll go pick it up! I think it is a fish.'

He waded into the water. It was a fish. He smelt it. It was fresh, lovely. He ran back to the shade, 'Dad, Dad! Look what I found. A fish!'

'Yo,' said the father. 'Cook it for us. The fire is there.'

'Also I got lots of sand crabs for you, for bait,' said Djet.

So he started cooking the fish. He turned it to the other side. When it was cooked, he got the leaves of the casuarina tree, the *djomala*, and used them as a plate. Then he started eating. His father was still making a spear. His father called out, 'How is it?'

'It's good. It tastes really fresh.'

Djet kept eating. Then his father said, 'Yo. Can I have the head of the fish?'

The son said, 'No, I did not find this for everyone. Plus it tastes a bit off. A bit rotten.'

He kept eating, kept eating. His father said, 'Son, can I have the tail?'

The son said, 'No, it is a bit small. Plus it tastes too rotten.' He kept eating.

'Yo, son, can I have the bones?'

'No, Father, I think it is really rotten. I can smell it.'

Finally, the father said, 'My son, can I eat the gills?'

'No,' said Djet. 'This part is the really rotten one. I can smell it. It tastes really bad.'

He ate it all up. He was a greedy son. He threw the bones in the sand for the crabs to eat.

'OK, Dad, I will go and play now. I have finished, I had to eat.'

His father was waiting for the tide to turn. As soon as it turned he called out to his son. 'Yo, son, I am going fishing now. You wait here.'

The father got into a big canoe and went off. He speared all sorts of fish. He caught *lalu* (parrotfish), *maranydjalk* (stingray), and all sorts. The boy ran off to get logs and firewood and made a big fire. He could see his father coming back.

His father waved and the boy knew he had a lot. He ran up to his grandfather, calling, 'My father is coming back. He got lots of fish!'

The canoe came up and the boy said, 'You got lots. You are a good fisherman.'

'Yes, I know,' said his father. 'Help me carry the *guya* and the *maranydjalk* up to the fire and we will cook them so that they will be ready when your grandmother and mother and sister come back.'

Djet helped carry all the fish and stingray up to the fire and the grandfather started cooking them. Grandfather cooked them on top of a beautiful big bed of ash.

Then little Djet pulled one out from the fire. 'I think I'll taste this one,' he said.

The father hit him on the wrist with a long stick. 'No, you are not to eat anything yet.'

He turned them to cook the other side. Djet went to pick another one but the father hit him on the hand. He said, 'No, you are not to eat yet.'

Djet thought, 'Maybe when it is all cooked, maybe that is the time to start eating.'

Finally the food was cooked. They took everything out. It was all prepared, all ready now. The pieces of stingray were kneaded and the liver was mixed in. Everything was ready for eating. The father and the grandfather started eating the stingray and the fish. Djet asked again, 'Can I eat now? One fish? Father?'

But his father said, 'No, I'm sorry, son, but you are not to eat any fish or any stingray.'

'Why, Father, why?'

The father said, 'Son, when I asked you for just a little bit of fish from the one you found, you said no. So my son, I am going to say no to you. You are not allowed to eat anything.'

Djet started crying. He cried and cried and cried. The grandfather and father ignored him. He cried so much that his little eyes started getting red and his nose started to grow. His arms were starting to grow feathers. He changed into a sea eagle. He flapped and flapped around, still crying. He flew off into the air.

The father saw him flying off and he started to feel sorry. 'My poor son. What have I done?'

At that moment, the mother, the sister and the grandmothers came back from gathering *ganguri*.

'What are you looking at?' they asked.

'My son. That's him.' He told the story to them. 'That's him now,' he said.

For that they all turned into big anthills: the sister, the mother, father, grandfather, all of them. They are still looking up and pointing, 'That is my son.'

They are still there.

That is why the eagle eats only raw fish now. He does not eat cooked ones any more. He eats raw fish. And still today, if you go to Yilpara you will see the anthills there on the coast looking out to sea. The moral of the story is that we must share. Whatever we catch, we share with people. Don't be like Djet.

The give-and-take of sharing

Wetj is sharing, the responsibility to share. It is a promise, a commitment, to share, to connect to certain people. Yolŋu people have had *wetj* from way back. Children are still coming up and learning *wetj*. It is still going on.

There is a cycle of *wetj*. Every time a man goes out hunting, if he gets *garrtjambal*, red kangaroo, or *guya*, fish, he gives some to his mother, father, his family. This is his responsibility. *Wetj* means gift, but a gift that you have the duty to give. The cycle of *wetj* means the connection goes both ways. You give but you also will receive. There's a story about this.

The story of a giant and two turtle-hunters

There were two brothers that were turtle-hunters. They always used to go out and hunt turtles for their community. But they knew that there was a giant that lived on an island and this giant used to go and terrorise the community, demanding their *miyapunu*.

'If you don't give me *miyapunu*, the whole turtle, I will kill you,' the giant would say.

That giant was called Yuwu Yuwutj.

One day the clan were having a ceremony. It wasn't turtle season, so turtles were scarce, but the clan said to the two hunters, 'You need to go further, further out into the

deep sea to catch turtle.' Only
these two brothers knew how
to harpoon the turtle. Before
they left they said, 'Because we
know Yuwu Yuwutj will smell
that *miyapunu*, come and look
for us if we don't return before
nightfall.'

So they collected their
miyapunu tools and off they
went, paddling, paddling past
that island where that Yuwu
Yuwutj lived.

'*Wawa*, brother, what are
we going to do if we don't find
miyapunu?' asked the elder brother.

'Don't worry, big brother, we'll find one. I know a place
where they gather to mate.'

Paddling, paddling, paddling. You could see the *miyapunu* on the horizon, their heads going up, down, splashes
everywhere.

'Little brother, *wawa*, you're so clever,' said the elder
brother.

Paddling, paddling. The brothers got to the place of the
miyapunu and the *miyapunu* weren't frightened. The turtles
were busy now, their mind was not on anything.

Little brother said, '*Wawa*, which one should we get?'

Big brother said to the little brother, 'You choose the
biggest one.'

43

Little brother looked around and he chose the biggest one. It was a green turtle, *marrpan*, the biggest he could see.

'Yo, yo!'

They got the harpoon ready and put the rope in place because the turtle was so big.

Big brother was teaching. He said, 'It's your turn now, you're the one who's going to spear this one, it's time to learn.'

The little brother launched the harpoon at the big green turtle. The harpoon shot into the water and into the shell. The big brother took the end of the rope and tied it to the canoe. The harpoon was in the turtle's shell and the little brother was holding on to the rope and letting it out. The turtle swam, then came up for air, dragging the canoe along behind – going, dragging, swimming everywhere, until it got tired and then they pulled it in and got it into the boat.

The turtle was dragged into the boat, and the big brother was so proud of the little brother. He said, 'You've done really well. I want you to teach the young boys now.'

They were happy. Canoeing, canoeing back now.

But Yuwu Yuwutj smelt them when they went past his island.

'Ahhhhhhhhhhhhhhhmmmmmmmmmmmmmm! *Marrpan*. Smelling *marrpan*!'

The land was shaking, like an earthquake, with him waking up. The two brothers were talking away, paddling away, they didn't notice.

'Waaaaa! Turtle! That's my turtle!'

Then splash, splash, splash, that giant was in the water.

44

He grabbed the canoe and dragged it. The two brothers cried out, 'Waaaaa, he found us!'

Yuwu dragged the canoe ashore.

'Please, you can't do this,' said the brothers, 'It's for all the people. They're hungry. We're having a ceremony. If you want we can go and get you some more tomorrow.'

'No, no. I'm eating now.' And he picked up the *miyapunu* and chomped it all up, throwing shell and everything into his mouth.

'I want some more, go and get me some more. Where did you find it?'

'We won't tell you where we found it.'

'If you don't I'm going to eat you.'

Yuwu just picked them up and ate them, swallowing them. Then he cried out, 'Oooooooooooooh, I wasn't meant to eat the people. Oooooooooooooh!'

His tummy was aching now. 'What have I done? What have I done?'

He lay down in pain.

Back at the camp, all the clan – men, mothers, sisters – were waiting. Waiting, waiting, waiting.

'What has happened?' they asked. 'Tomorrow we have to go and look for them.' They knew something bad had happened to them.

Morning came and everyone got up because of a sound. *Djooooooo!* It was the Yuwu farting. *Djooooooo!*

'Let's see what the Yuwu ate.'

Lots of canoes went to the islands. All the men went. It was a search party. They came to the island and the beach.

'That Yuwu farting, maybe he ate those brothers,' they thought. He was still sleeping, that Yuwu, still farting and rolling around. *Djooooooooooo!* The men, they crept up.

'What are we going to do? He's in pain, he can't do anything. Let's kill him.'

All these men jumped out from everywhere and started chopping into him, killing him. And they got to his stomach and the brothers were there. They were barely alive but they were still breathing. The other men got the brothers out and made a huge fire and threw Yuwu in it. They got the boys out alive.

Now the boys can get whatever *miyapunu* they want. They don't have to worry about that Yuwu. Before, they had been terrified. They'd always had to get two *miyapunu*, one for them and one for him. Now they can just go out and get one for the family as they need to.

When my grandmothers
collected food, they saved it in a
basket and shared it. Now we are putting
our knowledge in the basket and we are sharing
it – mother to grandchildren – and then
you can share it with your family.

LAKLAK BURARRWANGA

Laklak's Story 2

SCHOOL AND STORIES: GROWING UP IN YIRRKALA

I told you about walking to Yirrkala, to the mission school. I was excited to be there. It was so different from the bush at home. There were shops with things I'd never seen before, and family I'd never met. I wasn't in school yet. I spent the days with my family.

My mum was the eldest in her family. My mum's dad was a powerful and important Gumatj leader. And there was Dr Roy Marika, who became my dad. Roy Marika raised us up. I called him Bäpa, Dad. He was an amazing man, and a leader in the land-rights movement. We lived with Bäpa and his sons and daughter. I was like a little mother to the youngest ones, helping Mum change their nappies and looking after them.

I remember one time when Bäpa went to Brisbane to learn how to make fishing nets. He brought us back presents, dresses and biscuits and lollies. We had never tasted food like that before.

We lived in a tin house on the beach. Everyone was living on the beach in those days. Our house was a real long one with a wall down the middle. We lived on one side of it and three or four other families lived on the other side. It was an empty room and the floor was just sand. Every now and then we used to bring back clean sand from the beach and chuck it around and smooth it out. The smell of it was just beautiful.

The house had huge windows too, and we had a stick to prop them open. At night, we used to take the stick out and close the windows up.

We had a fire inside in one corner, usually near the door, where the cooking things were. The spaces along the walls were for sleeping. And the middle was for gathering, sitting down, like a living room.

The washing was done in the river. Everyone used to wash in the river. Swim in the river, wash in the river. The sea was in front of the house, and behind us were the mangroves and the fresh water. So we had the mangroves as our playground, and the beach.

I said before that my mum was pregnant when we walked to Yirrkala. Not long after we arrived, my youngest sister, Banbapuy, was born, next to the river, by the mangroves. Mum was very sick but I was there to help her. All of us in the family looked after her.

Then I started at the missionary school. We weren't allowed to use our language in the classroom. It was English all the time. If we spoke Yolŋu in the classroom, even one word, we were made to drink soap. Oh, the taste of soap! The soap was there soaking every day when we got to school in the morning. If we talked in language, they made us drink the thick, soapy water.

People at that missionary school, they were trying to change us. It was like brainwashing. The missionaries talked about marriage, they didn't like girls to marry too young and they said you had to get married in a church. We used to sing 'God Save the Queen'. And they would raise the flag, two boys would play drums and we would all line up and march into the classroom. We would salute the flag. True!

There was lots of punishment at that school. They smacked our hands, our bum, our legs. They made us stand on one foot in the corner – maybe for an hour. But not speaking our language, that was the worst. They were trying to demolish our language, really trying hard. But we are strong.

At that time the old people began to talk about bilingual education. They began a fight so that we could learn in two languages, English and Yolŋu Matha. This helped bring Indigenous languages into schools in a lot of Aboriginal communities. There was one teacher, Miss Ross, who became a linguist. With help of one of my mums she worked on translating the whole Bible into Yolŋu. Through her and the old people, the fight for bilingual education got going. The Yolŋu are still fighting for that.

We used to go off hunting after school. Not with our parents, just on our own. We were eight, nine, ten years old. We used to go hunting for yams, or for figs or munbi, a vine vegetable, or we'd go fishing with a fishing line and if there was no fishing line we would use cotton with a hook. And we would catch little ones, and cook and eat them. And sometimes we would bring some home for our family and they'd say, *'Ah, marrkap'mil'* ('Ah, my beloved!')

At weekends, when there was no work, everyone, the whole family, went off hunting together for bigger things like crabs, turtle, *rakay* (waterlily bulbs) and oysters.

Sometimes we'd go out with our grandmother to get *gunga* (pandanus leaves for weaving), and while we were getting *gunga* our grandmother would hunt for other things. All the time she told us stories and what to eat and what not to eat, and she showed us how to find all the bush foods. She taught us to hunt and told us stories, what things are wrong and what things are right; so we learnt the *Rom* (the Law).

I am *buku dhawu*. That means I really love listening to stories. Every time the old people told stories, I always listened carefully. I'd go with my parents, my grandmothers, the old people, and learn from them. Not like reading in a book, real thing! Like going out hunting, getting *ŋatha* (bush foods) or whatever. My brothers and sisters see me as not just a sister but as a mother, because I am the eldest and I learnt as much as I could.

3

Banumbirr,
THE MORNING STAR
Astronomy and Space

Look up at the pre-dawn sky. It is quiet and the wind is still. It is early, early morning and the stars are still bright. Soon Banumbirr, the morning star, will come over the horizon. Sit here with us and listen to the sound of clapsticks in the darkness. We're about to start an important ceremony.

Banumbirr helps us to contact our loved ones who have passed away. She is the link between us and Burralku, the island where our loved ones have gone.

There are three Banumbirr, in fact, three special morning stars. The first goes to a place called Dhambaliya; the second goes to Balaybalay. The third stands above Witiyana and Gundalmiri and shows the exact place where the sun will rise. So Banumbirr – or Venus – tells us that dawn will come: a new day, a new beginning

Today, we'll talk to you about our understandings of astronomy and space. Space is not empty for us, it is full of meaning. The stars are part of our world. They are all bound up with how it was created. They tell us things too. But first we will take you through the ceremony of Banumbirr and help you understand what it means to us.

Preparing for the ceremony

Preparation for the Banumbirr ceremony takes a long time. The men know that someone, a Dhuwa person, passed away a few years before and it is time for the renewal of their spirit. The men get together and talk about it. They then go to each community and let the extended family know what is going to happen.

The ladies start their preparations. We have to make the string for the beautiful morning star and ceremonial pole that will be used in the ceremony. It might take us a week to make the string for Banumbirr – to get that *dawu*, that fig-tree fibre, and make the sacred object, the Banumbirr. We'll explain to you how it's done. It's part of the behind-the-scenes work.

It starts at that *dawu*, that fig tree, where we hold the ceremony. We go out and collect *dawu* strings, the roots that hang down. Have you seen them? They are thin aerial roots dangling down like vines from the big old tree. We get those roots, nice straight ones. We heat them up, stretch them, hit them and grind them to get the inside of the vine. Then we open the side of the vine to scrape him out and finally we dry him on the sand.

After that, we rub it on our legs. We roll and roll it on our thighs, and this weaves the strands together to make a string. It's like spinning wool, only it's with the *dawu* fibre. We add more and more, and it grows and grows. We wake up early in the morning and start, and at lunch we're still working. If it's urgent, we'll make string all day until we have a big bunch.

The timing of the ceremony depends on the position of Banumbirr in the sky, the orbit of Venus you might say in Western knowledge. We mostly hold it during Rrarrandharr, maybe September or October, because the weather is dry then. It's an important ceremonial time. Rrarrandharr is the time of year when your feet burn when you walk on sand. It is very hot, before the rains come. Fruits are ripening in the sun. The stringybark is in flower. It's a bountiful season. *Bukmak*, everything, is ripening and getting fat: the *namura* (black-lipped oysters), *djinydjalma* (crab), *maranydjalk* (stingray) and different fruits. The *warrkarr* flowers are out now. The *warrkarr* is a white lily that grows at ground level in sandy places and is a very important flower for us. When the *warrkarr* is flowering, it is time for stingray. *Warrkarr* tells us it is stingray season. It's still *miyapunu* season too.

The word 'Banumbirr' refers to the actual morning star, but it also refers to the ceremony, the song and to the

57

beautiful pole that we make. The men cut a pole from a tree and put a group of feathers on the top, using beeswax. It is round, with the feathers fanning out to make a star. Inside the feather star it is colourful – red, orange, blue, green, just like a morning star. Then there are some white feathers, from the cockatoo. It's a big one. It's beautiful. We make the special string and interweave it with feathers, feathers from the rainbow lorikeet, from parrots and from other birds – seagulls, cockatoos. Any feather.

It might seem confusing to use the same name for the star, the songline, the ceremony, the ceremonial pole and the group of feathers, as well as the little poles for the children, the Dhangdhang. But to us, they are the same. The objects are a part of the ceremony, they are part of the sacred story. The ceremony is a part of the star. The star is part of the objects. So they are all 'Banumbirr'.

Keeping a loved one with us always

Everyone comes from far around to attend the Banumbirr ceremony. It is an important one. This ceremony is for those loved ones who have passed away. That Banumbirr we made, the morning star, it represents a Dhuwa person, their spirit. In a similar way Yirritja people make a Djurrpun, named for Spica, an evening star. They have their own connection through space to their ancestors. For Dhuwa, two or three years after someone passes away we make a Banumbirr for their spirit. We give that Banumbirr to the loved one's close

relations. The Banumbirr helps keep that loved one with them always. They carry it with them. They keep it in their house. It is a returning of the spirit of that loved one to their closest family members.

When we are ready to pass that Banumbirr on, we hold a big ceremony. All the different tribes come down from different communities, different homelands. We send a message stick or we ring on the phone.

The *manikay*, the song and ceremony, goes for one and a half weeks. The men sit under the *dawu* tree with the Banumbirr for the men's ceremony. During the last couple of days there is dancing and then on the last night the men and boys present the Banumbirr, the pole. The men sing and dance the night before. They might take a rest at 1 a.m. and then rise again at 4 a.m. to begin the final part of the ceremony. The women, they sit up all night – it's like a vigil. They sit in a group, waiting. The children doze on and off. They will wake excitedly when the moment comes.

The singing takes a lot of skill and knowledge. The men start early in the night but they finish their song at precisely the right time to coincide with the rising of the morning star, Banumbirr. They have to get the timing right. Imagine singing all night and knowing to the exact moment when a star will rise, then timing your song to end at that moment. That's what the men do. That's deep knowledge.

It's a songline from the star that the men sing. They sit under the *dawu* and sing the colour of the morning star, Banumbirr, describing how it is when the colour is coming up and lighting the trees.

Dancing at dawn

Listen! We can hear the clapsticks of the men. It must be time. Everyone's waiting and ready. Then the *yidaki*, the didgeridoo, plays. We hear the *yidaki* in the dark. Everyone gets up and gets ready. The sound of the *yidaki* lets women and children know that the Banumbirr is rising. It's a sign. The sound of the *yidaki* calls out for Dhuwa people to sit down and cry for the new Banumbirr, the new spirit of the person who passed away.

Imagine the stillness. Dawn is just breaking. We're all up, we've been up all night waiting for this special moment. It's beautiful out in the pre-dawn. Then look, see that flash of white? It's gone. It's dark again. No, wait, look, there it is again. They're bringing out the Banumbirr, the morning-star pole. You don't see people or anything, it's dark and we blend in with the darkness. You just see the white coming and going again, emerging from the darkness. Maybe it is the spirit itself that shows the Banumbirr.

Show and dance, show and dance. Out comes the pole Banumbirr. We look up and the star is there, Banumbirr, big, colourful and beautiful. The men are painted with red ochre before the ceremony. All the women have special painting on them too. They paint themselves to see Banumbirr. The children too. It's the Law. The Law says who should paint, to bring the spirit, the spirit of the extended family connected to the Banumbirr. The immediate family, Dhuwa and Yirritja, are painted with ochre too, painted with the red ochre for the spirit to come back to the people. Red ochre is sacred ochre, it makes you free so you can walk anywhere, it represents your mother and father.

The men use the Banumbirr, the pole, to show directions. One man is in the middle and he is telling the directions of the homelands. He names Dhambaliya and shows that way. He names Balaybalay and shows that way, then Witiyana and Gundalmiri. Every corner of Australia, each corner of Arnhem Land, is indicated: north, south, east, west. Banumbirr shows the directions.

The men dance with the Banumbirr. Show and dance, show and dance. Out comes the Banumbirr, and the singing and dancing moves into a different phase. It lasts until day-time, until 6 or 7 a.m. By now, all have joined in. We are

all dancing together, men, women, boys and girls, taking turns with Ba̲numbirr, the pole, the morning star.

To end the *manikay* we give the pole of Ba̲numbirr, the spirit, to the Dhuwa loved ones. They dance, and all the women come together and they cry. That is the end of the songline about Ba̲numbirr, when we give the Ba̲numbirr pole to the family.

The women cry, they sing their keening song. When they finish, they come crying, holding the pole, and give it to family, the Dhuwa loved ones, who will receive it. The Ba̲numbirr represents their father or their mother. Now the spirit of the person who died and the spirit of the family are connected.

This ceremony always ends with sunrise, the beautiful sunrise. Every time it is a different colour. To end, the men sound the clapsticks and the women cry the Ba̲numbirr song. The song describes the journey that a person must take as they go to the island of Burralku where the spirits live.

Ngamangamayun nyin Banumbirr
burralkubaym, butjuminggan.
Banumbirr ngunhuku ngathundawu.
Gunḏalmirriwu yaththawungu ditjuma
nyäku Banumbirr

62

Wäŋawu Ngaymilwu
Mäka dawuŋa Banumbirr
buku nyinhan
Wäŋa Ngaymilnha
djinaku yatawu
Banumbirr.

Making the Banumbirr pole.
The place called Burralku.
Putting feathers that will rise,
That come to the place and will stop
    at Gundalmiri.
Bring back my new Banumbirr, my spirit,
    tribe of Ngaymil people
That will stand Banumbirr at the fig tree.
All the Dhuwa clan will sit down under the fig tree
And cry and sing the coming
Of the new spirit of Banumbirr.

Place of the dead

The ceremony has ended but we'll spend the rest of today telling you more about Banumbirr and our connection to our dead. The spirit people live on Burralku. Burralku is an island out there where all Dhuwa spirits live, dance and make culture. Burralku is a place of the Dhuwa dead. Those spirits send Banumbirr the star to us, to north-east Arnhem Land. That's how the star comes; she is sent by our loved ones. They are making the stars and sending them over to us.

Banumbirr is the link between us and those loved ones on Burralku who have passed away. Through her they touch us and communicate with us. Banumbirr, the morning star, has a string trailing behind her. Along that string we send messages to our loved ones on Burralku. We are still doing that. The string keeps Banumbirr close to the sun as well. Did you know Banumbirr always stays close to the sun? That string is also the way the spirits go on their journey from this land to Burralku when they die.

Have you had someone close to you die? If you had, after a few years you would get this special Banumbirr, the morning star, to hold close to you. Perhaps you can imagine how you would feel. Think of the morning star and imagine how every morning you would wake up and see it and feel healed inside. You know the spirit who has passed away is with you, looking down on you and caring for you still. That spirit is in the object, in the artwork made of fig-tree string and feathers, and in the star itself.

We hope you can wake up early and see the star. When you wake up at 4.30 or 5 a.m. you can see the morning star. It makes you feel beautiful inside, like the Banumbirr.

It's happy and sad, this ceremony. When you think of your sisters or mothers or fathers who have passed away, you cry. And yet you also feel happy to have family and feel close to those who have passed away. We are happy that we are part of this.

Banumbirr's journey

Banumbirr came from the sea on a journey. On this journey she named things as she travelled, creating a songline through Arnhem Land and beyond Arnhem Land to the west. Banumbirr comes from the east, from Burralku, and passes over us in north-east Arnhem Land, heading to the west and connecting all the clans and people of Arnhem Land. So Banumbirr connects us too, all the clans who live under the arc she makes across the sky. At dawn, Banumbirr returns once again to Burralku. This is a Yolŋu songline, a songline connected to the land, the songline of Banumbirr.

In this ceremony we cry and think of the old people sending Banumbirr. The spirits are on Burralku and the bones are in the land. That is the Yolŋu way. The Mokuy, spirit people, send Banumbirr to us from Burralku.

The ceremony needs a deep knowledge of the working of the stars, and of time. As we said earlier, the men have to sing so that their song ends precisely as Banumbirr comes over the horizon. But there is other timing involved too. Did you know Banumbirr rises only a few hours ahead of the sun at certain times? That means we need to plan the ceremony carefully, and hold it at the right time so that Banumbirr can be seen heralding the coming of the dawn. We know the complex pattern of Banumbirr, her different paths throughout the year. Those different paths mean that she looks different sizes (and different colours too). Sometimes she is so large and so bright she casts a shadow like the moon. Other times she is small and far off. We have explanations for that. Some of them are sacred, like the stories of the dead. Some of them are simpler, like the bedtime story for children that we tell later on.

Nothing is empty

This ceremony, and the way we link the stars with the *dawu* tree, with ourselves and our loved ones, with song and dance, with the Law and with sacred stories, it shows how everything is linked together. People are not set apart from Nature; the earth is not separated from the sky; songs and stories are not separate from people and objects. All these things exist as part of one another. It is a form of relativity. Scientist Albert Einstein said that objects and energy are

different forms of the same thing. Our story and his story about the universe are similar. We hope you can see that with this story of Banumbirr.

In the Yolŋu world, we don't see space as empty or as somehow unchanging. There is a dynamism there in the sky, and between the sky and people. Nothing is empty to a Yolŋu way of thinking. Everything has a presence, and everything has an impact on us. It is not just flowing one way, as if people are the only ones who can act. The environment is not just a backdrop to people's actions. No, it's not like that. Animals, the land, the sky, the stars, the wind, everything is related to us, everything has an intelligence and can do things that affect us.

But that is enough for now. We've talked about a lot today. The *djäpana* is starting. Let's get the children to bed early tonight. It won't be hard to get them to sleep, they are so tired.

Come on, now, Merrki's going to tell you a story. This is a bedtime story for bigger children, for seven- or eight-year-olds. We'll tell it to you now to finish off our day together. It's another story about Banumbirr.

A story of spirits in the sky

One night a long time ago, there was a family. The mother was trying to put her baby to sleep. This was the first baby, the first baby on this earth. She was trying to get it to sleep, but that baby was upset over something. The baby cried and cried.

The mother cradled the baby. She sang a lullaby, but nothing worked. That baby just cried and cried and cried.

The spirits in the sky felt really bad. One spirit said, 'We need to help that mother, but what can we do? We can't just appear to her. That would make her frightened. I'll make a toy, a Banumbirr.'

That Banumbirr was really bright and really colourful.

It went from red to green to blue, orange and yellow. This was the morning star, Banumbirr. And the spirits made this really strong string to dangle from the sky to the earth for the baby to see.

The spirits started dangling that Banumbirr. From earth it looked really small, and then it got bigger and bigger and bigger, and the closer it got to earth the bigger it got. And it was changing colours. The mother didn't see this. She was cradling the baby, giving it *mimi*, breastmilk. The baby was looking into the sky. Banumbirr was right in front of the baby now, really big, and colours were changing and the baby stopped crying.

And then the spirits pulled it back up so it was getting smaller, smaller, smaller, and then when the baby started crying again they let Banumbirr down again and it looked bigger, bigger. The baby stopped crying. Then Banumbirr went up again and then down again and up and down until the baby fell asleep. So now we still see that some days Banumbirr is big, and some days she is really, really small. That is the spirits in the sky.

And when we dance that *mokuy*, the special ceremony for the spirits, we make Banumbirr with the feather and dance Banumbirr getting bigger, or smaller. You can hide it behind your back and when the baby cries you show it to her.

Our dillybag (*gay'wu*)
vision holds all women and
families, our country, our culture,
our knowledge and our stories.

LAKLAK BURARRWANGA

Laklak's Story 3

A HUGE HOLE IN OUR COUNTRY: MINING AND LAND RIGHTS

In the early 1960s, bauxite (aluminium ore) was discovered near Yirrkala. That changed our life. The government in Canberra approved a mine to go ahead up here without even talking with us. They just talked to the head of the Methodist mission overseas and that was all the consultation they thought they needed. Back then, Arnhem Land was an Aboriginal reserve and we weren't recognised as owners of the land, so we didn't have a say. Aboriginal people weren't recognised by the white law at all. There weren't any land rights. We weren't even counted in the census. We weren't seen as citizens.

A lot of Yolŋu were pushed off the land to make room for the mine. The company – Nabalco – came in with bulldozers, trucks and other machinery and destroyed sacred land of our clan and our people. They cut down trees, bulldozed plants and animals, and drove other animals away. But we depended on that Country for our life, our food and our culture.

When we went hunting we'd hear their car come, and someone would call, 'Miners! Miners!' and we'd run and hide. 'Lie flat down,' we were told by our parents. And I remember shaking like hell. I didn't know why we were lying down. We were told they were bad men.

I remember the old people taking us to see a huge hole being dug in our Country and them telling us this is steel, this will be steel for buildings. And I remember my sister Merrki saying, 'How? How do they do that? This is just rock.'

CREATION STORIES AND THE CHURCH PANELS

Our grandparents wanted to tell the government, the mission and the company how important the land was for us. They wanted the government people to understand that it was our place, that we are part of our place and it is part of us. Our grandparents, Yirritja granddad and Dhuwa granddad, Mungurrawuy Yunupiŋu and Mawalan Marika (Bäpa's eldest brother), organised for all the clans to come in and make some big panels of sacred paintings. The panels, one Dhuwa and one Yirritja, showed the creation stories, the Law, of Yolŋu Country. They were an important way of us showing our sovereignty. Those panels use our sacred paintings and Law to say, 'This is Yolŋu Country, we have a deep connection with this Country, it is our kin and we have rights and responsibilities here.' It's about who we are, where we are. And it's a claim to this place.

The Church panels are still here. If you visit Yirrkala and come to the Art Centre, you can see them. They're important not just to us but also to the history and meaning of this country, Australia. Some people say those panels are among the most important Aboriginal art ever created.

TELLING OUR ANGER: THE BARK PETITION

At the time the panels hung in the church in Yirrkala, and that was good, a sacred thing, but people didn't realise their

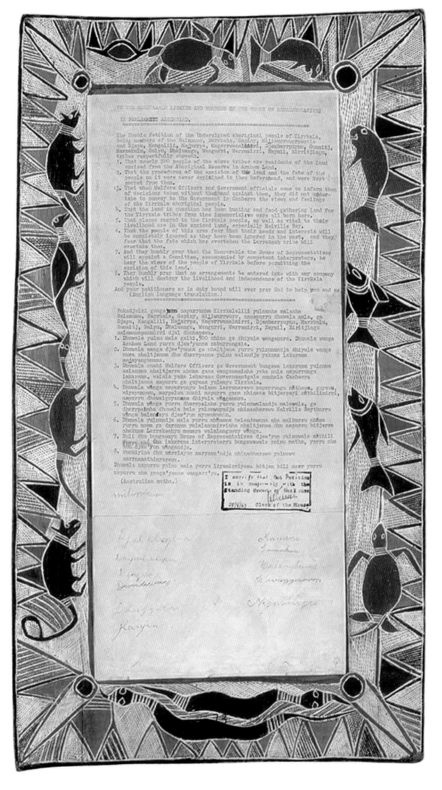

TO THE HONOURABLE THE SPEAKER AND MEMBERS OF THE HOUSE OF REPRESENTATIVES
IN PARLIAMENT ASSEMBLED.

The Humble Petition of the Undersigned aboriginal people of Yirrkala, being members of the Balamumu, Narrkala, Gunmulal, Milikawarrpan and Djapu, Mangalili, Mrkarpuy, Kagarrauwul—tiarr; Djamarrpuyna, Gumaitj, Marrakulu, Galpu, Dhalianawuy, Wangurri, Warramirri, Maymil, Miritjigung, tribes respectfully sheweth,

1. That nearly 500 people of the above tribes are residents of the land excised from the Aboriginal Reserve in Arnhem Land.
2. That the procedures of the excision of the land and the fate of the people on it were never explained to them beforehand, and were kept secret from them.
3. That when Welfare Officers and Government officials came to inform them of decisions taken without them against them, they did not undertake to convey to the Government in Canberra the views and feelings of the Yirrkala aboriginal people.
4. That the land in question has been hunting and food gathering land for the Yirrkala tribes from time immemorial; we were all born here.
5. That places sacred to the Yirrkala people, as well as vital to their livelihood are in the excised land, especially Melville Bay.
6. That the people of this area fear that their needs and interests will be completely ignored as they have been ignored in the past, and they fear that the fate which has overtaken the Larrakeah tribe will overtake them.
7. And they humbly pray that the Honourable the House of Representatives will appoint a Committee, accompanied by competent interpreters, to hear the views of the people of Yirrkala before permitting the excision of this land.
8. They humbly pray that no arrangements be entered into with any company which will destroy the livelihood and independence of the Yirrkala people.

And your petitioners as in duty bound will ever pray God to help you and us.
(English language translation.)

====================================

Bukudjulil gonga napurrunha Yirrkalalili yulnanha malanha Balamumu, Narrkala, Gunmuy, Milikwurruwru, napnapurru Dhuwala mala, ga Djapu, Mangalili, Mrkarrpun, Kagarrawmaidmirri—tiarr, Djamarrpuyna, Marrkulu, Gumaitj, Galpu, Dhalianuy, Wangurri, Warramirri, Daymil, Miritjingu malamanapurralirri djal dinnapana.

1. Dhuwala yulnu mala galki, 500 dhina ga dhiyala wanganawa. Dhuwala wanga Arnhem Land yurru djan'yunna naburrungala.
2. Dhuwala wanga djan'yunna ga nhaltjana yurru yulnannandja dhiyala wanga nura nhaltjanna dha dharrpanna djalu walandja yakona lakarama nagayangunna.
3. Dhuwala wandi Welfare Officers ga Government bungawa lakarama yulnawa malanana nhaltjanna nhuna gana wangananandina yaka mala napurrungu lakarama, walala yaka lakarama Governmentgala nambala Canberra nhaltjanna napurru ga guyana yulnapu Yirrkala.
4. Dhuwala wanga napurrunyu balanu larrunarawa napurrungu nhuhawa, guywa, miyapunawa, marpalwa madhi napurru gana nhinana bitjarrayi nhaliminirri, napurru dharrpiyamana dhiyala wanganawa.
5. Dhuwala wanga yurru dharrpalaba yurru yulnamalandja malawala, ga dharrpalaba dhuwala bala yulnawagadja nhinanharawa Melville Baytharru wanga balandayi djan'yun nyununkunla.
6. Dhuwala yulnannila mala yurru nhananu balandawayna dha walkurra ninda yurru nowa ga darmuna yulnlanuwirirana nhaltjanana dha napurru bidjarra nhaluna Larrakeahgu nonara walalamanguway wanga.
7. Nuli dha bungawayi House of Representatives djan'yun yulnuwala nathili thuru—nuli dha lakarama interpreterru bungawawala yulnu matha, yurru nha djan'yun nangunija.
8. Nunhiyina dha nhirilawa marrana'ndja nhinanharawa yulnuwa narrananhthinarawa.

Dhuwala napurru yulnu mala yurru liyandariyama nhitjan bili naar yurru napurru nha ronga'yunna wangurri'a.

(Australian matha.)

[signatures]

I certify that this Petition
is in conformity with the
Standing Orders of this House
23/8/63   Clerk of the House

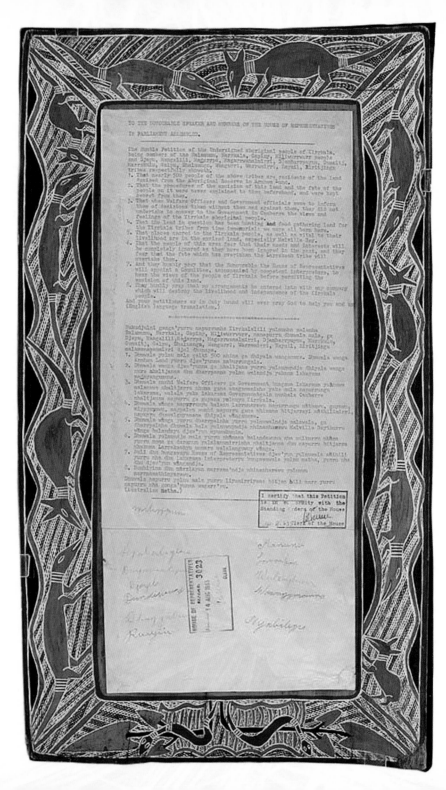

full meaning. The company didn't listen to the message. So Bäpa (my dad, Roy Marika) and our leaders decided that they needed to talk straight to the government and to make a direct protest about the mining. They wanted to lay claim to the land. So they made a special petition. It had bark paintings around the outside, with English and Yolŋu text in the middle. The paintings and the text together told the government about our relationship to the land and our anger about the mine. The Bark Petition is famous. It's an important part of the history of Australia and the fight for land rights for Aboriginal people.

In the end the Parliament did hear the petition. I remember the big dance in Canberra, the big ceremony when the government recognised the Bark Petition and Yolŋu Law. All the Elders came in to Yirrkala from their different communities and I was invited to dance there. I was the only girl who was invited to dance, with my mother and Bäpa. All Bäpa's brothers and sisters were dancing and singing because Bäpa was singing and dancing. It was a wonderful day, a wonderful thing that happened. It was the first time, see, that the government ever recognised Indigenous Law in Australia or even acknowledged our existence. Finally, our own culture and our own Law were being respected.

After all that there was a big meeting between the Nabalco and Gove people, but in the end nothing actually happened. The mining just kept on going. We had to keep struggling for justice.

Our family was very involved in trying to stop that mine and to claim rights over the land. Our house was called 'Land Rights House' because the meetings were held there. Our uncle was involved and our grandfather. Bäpa was the first man who could understand ŋapaki law and play the intermediary role. Whenever there was a meeting or an argument between Yolŋu and ŋapaki, Bäpa would be in the middle explaining and helping everyone to understand each other. At night-time he would tell us stories about long time ago, and then he'd teach us what would be the future for ourselves and our grandsons and granddaughters.

A BIG FIRST, BUT NO WIN: THE COURT CASE

In the end, our leaders took the case to the Supreme Court. That was a big first, the Milirrpum Case. It was a big thing for our claim to be taken seriously by the Court. The Court acknowledged our connection with Country and our long history here, but they did not recognise us as owning the Country. So we lost the case. Those men in Canberra, they ruled to let that mining go ahead and they denied us land rights.

Our old men gave the government men the bark paintings, telling them, 'This is our life, this is our land,' but they got nothing in return.

'Oh yeah, lovely, lovely,' those government people would say and get in their car, drive away back to their place to plan how to mine it, mine the land.

Now that you know about yothu-yindu and how the land is family to us, you can understand why we were trying to get our Country back and protect it. Every tree that might be cut down, every lizard that might be killed, every rock that might be ground up and taken away, *these all were our mothers and our children*. They are all Dhuwa or Yirritja, just like us. We are of our land and it is of us. Nabalco started mining, and it took part of us, killed our family.

The court case did show people how unfair Western law could be and made way for the Commonwealth legislation, the *Land Rights (Northern Territory) Act* of 1976. Aboriginal people got land rights thanks to the movement that started with the Church panels and the Bark Petition, thanks to my dad and other Yolŋu Elders. They've got that bark petition hanging at Parliament House in Canberra now.

Bäpa fought hard. He was so well respected for the way he worked between Yolŋu and *ŋapaki* law. He was recognised with an MBE. I did a painting and gave it to Bäpa, and he took it along to the Queen in England. He drew a picture and I did the painting and then he got the MBE at Buckingham Palace. He shook hands with the Queen and in a photo I saw my painting, with the Queen and Bäpa standing in front. *Latju ŋarraku* (my good) memories.

It was about this time, during the land-rights struggle, that I had my first baby, Djawundil, my daughter. I was young, still going to school. Early! Maybe I was sixteen years old. She was born with long hair, curly hair. A healthy baby.

And after birth we have a special secret women's ceremony. It is old women's Law. When the baby is born you can still get sick, so we have a special healing for the mother and baby. That is women's Law.

wäkun
makarrata gara

4

Gara, SPEAR

The sharp end of hunting and justice

We've had a relaxing day, so now let's go *walawi*, night hunting. We'll share a little of the men's business with you. Here's how it works. When men go hunting, when they catch a *miyapunu* or *djunuŋguyaŋu* (dugong), a *guya* or *maranydjalk* (stingray), they are looking, listening, feeling, all the time. Because they are part of the system and they understand the system, they are good hunters, they can see and understand the logic that holds it all together. We think of it as a kind of mathematics – a system of patterns and flows that make up our world.

There are lots of things the men know when they hunt: when to dive, what's heavy, what's light, which way to pull the rope, which way the *djunuŋguyaŋu, miyapunu* or *guya* will swim, how fast it will go. They know the colour of the animal, the colour of the water. And the shapes, they recognise and understand the importance of the shapes too – *miyapunu* or *djunuŋguyaŋu* shapes, different shapes for different *guya*, and *maranydjalk* – and the skin *(djunuŋguyaŋu* skin is very tough and tight). They know the pattern of the *gapu*, they know which is shallow water and which is deep water. That's the men's story.

It's November, and this year it's now the season of Worlmamirri here at Bawaka. It is the nose of the wet, the beginning of what *ŋapaki* call 'the build-up'. It's hot, even at night, and we might see some lightning flickering in the distance. The stringybark is in flower. It's night-time and we're sitting around having a yarn, *wanga*. Here is Leon. He is the only Yolŋu man out at Bawaka at the moment. Apart from him, we're all women. He wants to go night fishing for *wäkun* (mullet), and he needs someone to help. He needs a *bamara*, someone to be with. He asks Djawundil to come along. Do you want to go too?

We'll get a bag, the spears, a torch. We'll get in the car and drive to Bayini Beach.

It looks different at night-time, doesn't it? The trees are shadows. There is no moon tonight. That is the best time to hunt *wäkun*, in the new moon. The fish can't see so well. It will be dark and when we turn on the torch they will be hypnotised. And we know they are fat and ready to eat when the water is brown with scum on it. Everything has its time and place and good hunters know and understand times and places. They know how to understand the messages that are all around them.

It is important to hunt in the right season and to understand the signals. It is best to hunt *miyapunu* on a sunny day because you can see a lot better and it's easier to see through the water to spot the *miyapunu* and throw the *djambatj* (harpoon), to pierce the shell.

To be a good hunter you need a good *gara* (spear). *Benydjurr* is the kind of spear we are using tonight. It's the one to use for *wäku͟n*. There's no sharp wire point on the end of it. The end is just sharpened wood, shaved to catch the fish. See the spear lying in the troopie? That is *benydjurr*.

There are different types of *gara* and all *gara* are either Yirritja or Dhuwa. *Gayit* is the fighting spear, the shovel-nosed spear. Each group of men calls it by a different name. They use it for dancing, to make them strong and keep them powerful. They also use it for some big animals like *dhum'thum* and *garrtjambal*. *Wilmurr* is the fishing spear men use all the time, for everyday life. It has the wire point on the end and is good for *maranydjalk*. *Larrpan* is the ceremonial *gara* cut from the mangrove, a special tree. *Ganybu* is a *gara* used for freshwater fish, with a net made out of *dawu* string. When little kids first learn to throw they use *gaditjirri*. That's the long grass up on the point, the long grass that *dhimurru* winds lay flat when the mosquitoes go. The only way children learn to throw is by us showing them. We take them out and show them.

Coastal men, Bawaka men, love the *djambatj* (the harpoon) because that's their knowledge. They use the tall, skinny stringybark trees, the really straight ones, to make *djambatj*. Men know those have really strong power. Men who live by the sea are always thinking about using *djambatj* for *dhalatpu*, *djunuŋguyaŋu*, maybe *bäru* (crocodile). They love hunting, even if it is raining or cold. When they see little clouds drifting along the coastline, they know. These small clouds are messengers connected to the men. So when they see the clouds, the men think about the sea, they look towards the favourite places where the *djunuŋguyaŋu* go, where there's lots of food. Men know to check two types of sea grass floating on the water. If they've been cut cleanly, it's the hawk-billed turtle, *mudu̱thu*, at work. If they have been chewed up, *djunuŋguyaŋu* are in the area.

There are lots of stories connecting men and sea and Nature, trees and spears – lots of names and meanings. Many we can't talk about here. One deeper layer of understanding has to do with the role of the spear in justice. We'll tell you a bit about *gara* and justice now. But the use of spears can be ceremonial and those meanings are too deep to share with you here. You're only getting the top layer of the *raŋan* here in this book.

Justice the old way: *makarrata*

Makarrata is a peace-making ceremony where justice is done. Let me tell you a bit about our old style of justice. This

is used when there is a lawless person who has taken a wife from another man, someone who has done the wrong thing in ceremonies or committed cold-blooded murder. It is similar to having a court hearing. Once it is done, the case is over. *Makarrata* wipes the slate clean. Justice has been done.

Imagine there is a man who murdered my brother. The elders would say, 'Stop fighting to have the funeral.' The elders are the ones who dispense justice, who decide on the penalty. We would do the funeral first, pay the respects as we should. Then we would discuss where to hold the *makarrata*, the court. The older people would come and tell us, my brother's family, and the other family, the family of the murderer, when and where the revenge or the payback was to take place. The men would get their spears ready.

At the time and place, one of my other brothers would stand in for my murdered brother. My brother and the murderer would stand apart. They would measure the distance with their eyes. Our family would stand next to my brother. The murderer's people also have to stand there and get ready. All the men can watch. No children, no women, only men. All the women and children stay at home. My brother throws the spear. He has to aim at the leg and use a ceremonial spear. The murderer has to fall down on the ground. Then the murderer's family members pull out the spear and say, 'Now you are free.' They will take him home.

Next day, my family, the whole community, everyone together, comes to the other family. They make unity, peace.

This is our law as it once was. Maybe it is still used somewhere, but not here any more. Now we pass these matters on to the police, to be decided by the law of the government.

Maranydjalk and Bäru

Let us tell you where this came from, the idea of *makarrata*, justice. It started with a fight between Bäru, the crocodile, and Maranydjalk, the stingray. Both Maranydjalk and Bäru are Yirritja. They were fighting about who can live in the river at Birany Birany.

Theirs was a long argument. It went on a long, long time. Then Bäru the crocodile said, 'Let's make peace somewhere.'

So they went far away to the island where there is no one. The water took them very deep. This was deep ocean water called *manbuyŋa* that sweeps into a storm. They were still arguing the whole way while they were travelling. They travelled two hours, maybe three. The island was called Murrmurrnga. Murrmurrnga is another of my son Djawa's names.

There's a big rock standing in the water there. They sat. Bäru the crocodile said, 'We've been in an argument a long time. About that river, the water and the land. How about we make a peace? So the water will be calm. Crystal-clear, calm, at peace.'

Maranydjalk the stingray said, 'Bäru, you stand like this with your arms out.' He motioned for Bäru to stand with his front arms down, leaning forward. Maranydjalk came behind and used the barb on his tail to stab Bäru in the leg.

Bäru was jumping and shouting. While he was jumping and screaming, Maranydjalk said, 'Okay, mate, we will live here forever. We have made peace now. You will live on the top and turn into a rock shaped like a crocodile. I will live underneath.'

They are still there, they are the rocks. Everything there reminds us how to act now. The crocodile and the stingray, Bäru and Maranydjalk, made peace. Now there is peaceful water. The rock shape of the *bäru* is there and reminds us of the lesson. The Gumatj people still hold the song and the dance for this story; they hold the knowledge. This story is told by many people today.

Fishing for *wäkun*

But enough of the story for now. Here we are at Bayini Beach. Look, as we drive onto the beach you can see in the headlights of the troopie where the schools of *wäkun* (mullet) are. We all get out of the troopie and stretch our legs. Leon takes the torch and the *gara* and heads down towards the water. You men might want to take a *gara* or a torch and join him. Make sure you are quiet, though, or you will scare the fish.

We all walk along the edge of the water. Djawundil has the bag there on the sand, waiting. Leon and the men shine the torch around to see where the fish are, then quickly turn it off so it is dark. The fish are generally close in. The hunters step into the water, carefully, quietly. Sometimes they wade out to their knees. They know they mustn't scare the fish!

As the water is disturbed by the *guya*, the phosphorescence in the water lights up and this shows the hunters where the *guya* are. The hunters know which type of *guya* it is by the speed and the way it moves through the water.

Then someone shines the torch, a really bright torch to hypnotise the *guya* so they stay still. You can see the eyes of the fish because the water is so clear. One person holds the torch and shines it at the fish. Then the other spears it.

Spearing a fish takes great skill and an understanding of mathematics. All hunters use mathematics to know where to aim when spearing through the water. If the *guya* are staying in one spot to feed, the hunters don't aim at the *guya*, they aim closer to themselves. Where they aim always depends on how far the fish are below the surface. That's because the light is refracted, bent in water.

A moving target is even more difficult to aim for. You stand still and turn on the torch, and the fish come towards you. If they are moving, you must aim to the front of them, taking into account the speed of their movement. It's all about the timing. You have to take into account not just the refraction but the speed of the fish.

There, Leon throws his spear. He has a *wäkun*. And another. He hurls the fish to us on the sand. Djawundil hits them on the head with the *galpu*, the woomera, and puts them in the bag. It's teamwork. We will keep moving along Bayini Beach until we have enough. Sometimes the school of *wäkun* won't move too far away and you can follow it.

You follow the school or look for a new school.

There are different techniques too, different ways to work. For example, it's easier to get a *ŋuykal* (kingfish) if we run in front of it and wait for it to come to us. If you hit the head of the *ŋuykal*, it's down straight away. It dies instantly. But if you miss the head and it takes your spear, that's fine too. Your best chance is to hit the head. It is about accuracy in calculating angles and speed, distance and refraction.

For *miyapunu*, you have to be patient and wait; you can spear it only at a certain depth. Because a *djambatj* (harpoon) is buoyant, it doesn't keep on going down after it hits the water.

While we've been talking, we have moved down the beach towards the rocks. We now have ten *wäkuṉ*. It's time to go home. If we didn't have enough, we would go around to the other side of the beach and continue hunting; but we only take what we need. Let's go back to the troopie now. Will you carry the *gara*?

How a spear is made

Would you like to know more about the making of the spears? Men get *gara* from the land, and men belong to the land where the *gara* grows. They can get them from any country, in the jungle, by the sea. Two main trees used are *malwan* and *gutpa*. The men won't chop all the trees, they only take one or two, because they care for the land. Yolŋu have always cared for the land and Nature with their own knowledge.

Yolŋu knowledge is very important when men make *gara*. They look for a tree that is a good height. Then they use a special measurement. They hold their arms apart and measure the trunk from fingertip to fingertip. That makes the *gara* a good length, so it is right for the maker, whether he is short or tall. For *wilmurr* (that's the hunting spear), the *lirra* (prongs) must be even to make it strong. *Lirra* means the prongs on the end of the spear, but it can also mean 'tooth'. One word, different meanings. If you don't have a spear, you can just sharpen a stick from the *djomala* (casuarina) tree.

When men make *gara* they are thinking about getting fish from the sea. Hunting, getting food, is always on their mind. When non-Indigenous men visit Bawaka they are often taken hunting. They start to understand how to use a *gara* and to understand the mathematics that is so important for hunting.

Hunting stingray

If the *warrkarr* (the white lily flower that tells us that it is stingray season) is out, then the men will get their *wilmurr* ready. They might check that the *lirra* are sharp enough and if not they might use a file or large stone boulder to sharpen them to a fine tapered point. Then they'll jump into the troopie and head back down the road to hunt *maranydjalk* at Guluruŋa. The wide, shallow, mangrove-lined bay here is good for hunting *maranydjalk* and on the other side you can get good *ṉamura,* black-lipped oyster. At this time of year, big flat mud crabs can also be found and gathered.

If we were hunting stingray, a Yolŋu hunter might rub sweat from under his armpits all over your body and head. This is for your protection, so that Country will recognise you, so that Country will acknowledge and know you. It will protect you then. *Maranydjalk* the stingray will recognise the local scent and won't hurt you.

Low tide is best for *maranydjalk.* During low tide the water is shallow for a long way out and you can slowly make your way along the shoreline. The deep depressions on the sandy bottom tell you where the *maranydjalk* is lying. When the *maranydjalk* takes off, the sand is disturbed and you can see a cloudy trail. You won't get that trail if it is a shovel-nose shark lying on the bottom. The hunters spot the *maranydjalk* by looking for its shadow as it glides away. Yolŋu hunters know the shadow shape of the animals they hunt. They use the *galpu,* the woomera or spear-thrower, to help throw the *gara.* Once the *maranydjalk* is caught and

killed, you need to remove the poisonous barb in the tail so it won't hurt you. You hold the tail tightly between your teeth and rub a *galpu* down the length of the tail to break the barb off. You then get rid of it carefully so no one will stand on it. Men also use the *galpu* to hit the fish on the head and stun or kill it.

Songlines and fish traps

Men have their knowledge in the land, sea and Nature. They know where to get food so they can feed the family. And there's always a songline for men. Songlines play a very important role. For Yirritja men, there's Wurramala. He's *djambatŋu yirritjang*, meaning he's smart, he's an expert. He knows the tides of the sea, when they're going in and out. He knows that if the tide is coming in, there are probably lots of *miyapunu* and *djunuŋguyaŋu* – 'Let's go!' He knows everything, the water, where the food for *miyapunu* and *djunuŋguyaŋu* is, where they'll go.

People can sing the islands, they can sing clouds, and they can sing Wurramala, strong, tall Wurramala. He is the *bunguwa* (boss) who pulls the canoe, sings the canoe. He has his own knowledge and calls canoes and gets *djunuŋ-guyaŋu*. The *bunguwa* can sing the water and everything that is in the water or floating on the water like coconuts. He can sing paddling the canoe out to the islands, looking for *djunuŋguyaŋu*. The people can sing *djunuŋguyaŋu* and then they have to sing the harpoon and, yes, they sing the person

who stands to harpoon the *djunuŋuyaŋu*. And when they return, they sing about returning to the boat, seeing the *djunuŋuyaŋu*. There's a songline to sing the knife and guide them on how to cut up the *djunuŋuyaŋu*, and then afterwards, how to eat it. And then there's the end of the song, like the sunset, *djäpana*.

We also use Yolŋu knowledge to catch fish with a *yambirrpa*, a fish trap made with rocks. We lay all the stones in a group. As the tide goes out it leaves a pool inside the stones and the fish get trapped. This is knowledge that has been passed on from generation to generation. The old people knew everything, way back, and they passed it on to us through our grandparents, mothers, fathers, aunties, uncles, brothers and so on. And this keeps going, the knowledge passed on to use in everyday life, and it's still the one Law. There are lots and lots of different traps. That's just one.

We're back at camp now. The fish are on the fire. Leon has gutted them. Some are in the freezer. We will take them back to Yirrkala when we next head into town. Let's have a cup of tea while we wait for the *wäkuṉ* to be ready. And just as we end all songs with *djäpana*, we will end today with a story.

Hunting is men's business now but it wasn't always like that. Merrki will tell you a story of two sisters, the Two Sisters who named everything. The story tells how hunting used to be. This is just the top story. We're not going down deep. It's another story of the Djan'kawu sisters. Drink your tea, now, while you listen.

A story of the Djan'kawu sisters

The Djan'kawu were two sisters. They came from the sea, from deep water. When they came up to the surface there was a roar.

This is a story of the creation of life. The Djan'kawu sisters paddled in a canoe from that place in the sea. They paddled for days. They created fish, all the creatures of the sea. And they named everything in the water: the plankton, the micro-organisms, the whales. They reached the land at the long beach behind Bawaka. You can see the beach there, and on the beach the canoe (it's a rock now) where they came ashore.

They carried digging sticks with them and with those sticks they created fresh water, the springs. They stuck their sticks in the ground and fresh water came out. They created trees, plants, birds, food, animals.

You see a tree on the way to Bawaka, at Lirrina. The sisters sat there because on the other side it was too windy. They rested there before they started their journey east. The *larrani*, bush apples, from that tree are white. You can't eat that fruit. Only elders with grey hair, with knowledge, can eat from that tree; not young ones.

On the journey east the Djan'kawu created everything. The younger sister, she gave birth to all the Dhuwa clans. Not the Yirritja ones, they came later.

One day, they went hunting. They heard a crowd of men shouting.

'*Wei, yapa*, sister!' one of them said. 'What's happening? Let's go take a look.'

They rushed back to their camp. The saw the men taking their dillybags. When the men saw the sisters they ran off with the dillybags and those special digging sticks. They stole them.

When the Djan'kawu sisters saw what had happened they knew they had lost the power to create. They had lost the knowledge, the sticks that could create new life. And they'd lost the ability to hunt big animals.

Women still have the power to create life, through having babies, but only through babies. They can no longer create new plants, new fruits, new animals. Sometimes we wonder what other plants and animals there would be if those men hadn't taken those things!

With those sticks, the men got the knowledge to sing in public, and the laws that allow men to be at the head of the family. It gave them the power to hunt. But they didn't use the sticks to create.

I ask them, what's
this? They say, 'It's a basket'.
I say, it's not a basket, it tells a story.
It is a story, like a story in a book. But without
books, we have our hands – and the colours and
patterns in a basket are like letters, commas,
capital letters. They are the message. With the
different colours, the different stitchings,
you start from small up and up and up.
It's like going through the university.

LAKLAK BURARRWANGA

Laklak's Story 4

BACK TO OUR HOMELAND, BAWAKA

The mining at Gove helped start the homelands movement. It was heartbreaking for the Elders to see the destruction of their Country. The alcohol that came in with the miners was destroying us too. We had fought hard to stop the mine, but we'd lost, so we decided to move out of town (Yirrkala), away from the mission and on to the homelands. Other Indigenous groups were doing this too, and people began to talk about the 'homelands movement'. We wanted to keep our connections with the land strong, to maintain culture and ceremony. We wanted to be self-sufficient and to live the right way on Country, to be true to ourselves, our Country and our Law.

It was the early 1970s. Our family started spending time at Guluruŋa, on Port Bradshaw. Around this time I started work as an assistant teacher at the old school in Yirrkala. It was now a government school. I had three young children then. We'd go out to Guluruŋa at weekends to help clean up, and collect water from the borehole. My children grew up there. It was their childhood home.

Then we began to stay for longer times, not just for week-ends. Dad said we should start a business. We didn't call it a business then, but we made one anyway. When the tides were high we'd collect all the mangrove crabs, boil them and take them in the troopie to sell to Nabalco. We had an old-fashioned Toyota (it's still there at Guluruŋa). Dad loved the grandchildren. He'd take the boys for a ride – Ritjilili's son Rodney, my children Djawa and Aron, and the other kids. And the girls, Djawundil and Bayngala, would go too.

They used to drive to Gove and Dad would send the children inside. He'd tell them in English, 'You go in and ask the white boss, "Do you want crab?"' He'd be getting the kids confident, encouraging them to use English and to talk to *ŋapaki*. When the manager for Nabalco said yes, Dad would come in with the children to tell him how much to pay for the crabs. And they'd get the money and go to Yirrkala and get flour, sugar, tea bags and some lollies for the children. They'd go to the shop near the church where my sister Ritji was working.

One of the kids was Clinton. His dad was working at the mine but every weekend they'd come to Guluruŋa. He'd stay with us and ride on the truck with all the other kids. He was the first white child to meet black children. That's important to us.

That truck was the only vehicle we had to transport 20 people from the different clans and to get supplies to and from Yirrkala. Often we had to walk. It took seven hours to get from the community at Guluruŋa to the Dhupuma Indigenous College. From there you could take a bush taxi into Yirrkala.

By now we were staying at Guluruŋa most of the time. Dad thought that my two youngest sisters Banbapuy and Merrki should go to Dhupuma College to study teaching. Mum was a cleaner at the college at that time. But they were crying, they didn't want to go to school and stay by themselves. Anyway, they went, but at weekends they would all come back to Guluruŋa. Sometimes Dad worried about them. He'd go up Mosquito Creek in our dinghy and drive up to Dhupuma College to pick them up. They'd stay for the weekend and then he'd take them back up Mosquito Creek and radio the Principal to bring a vehicle to collect them.

I married my husband then. He was a landowner, a Gumatj man. His life was about independence. He loved going out with the dads, learning about culture. He talked a lot. He loved people, the same as my son Djawa/Timmy.

From our place at Guluruŋa, my husband's family started thinking about going to Bawaka. Bawaka is so lovely. The Burarrwangas, Yunupiŋus, Mununguritj families, the Gumatj families, we used to walk along the beach for two hours to get to Bawaka. While we walked, we collected our dinner – crabs and fruits – carrying a billycan of water, plus sugar and damper. We'd be talking with the kids. We'd go just for the day, looking at where to start the homeland.

We were staying at Bayini Beach first, but it's only a short beach so we walked to this side of Bawaka. The Mununguritj and Yunupiŋu families came first and started cleaning up the beach together. I remember walking with my three children. We started there, cleaning up Bawaka, cutting some trees for houses, building the houses, doing the ceremony, teaching the children Dhuwa and Yirritja and which is which country.

Lots of Yolŋu were involved in the homelands movement. Yolŋu were thinking of the future and of the new generation. My mum's family moved to Dhaniya then too, across the bay

from Bawaka. There was no road. They'd come to Bawaka
and then take a boat across the bay to the other side. We all
wanted our children and grandchildren and future Yolŋu to
know their Country, to know their homelands. We're still living
that movement, still living our past and our future together
here at Bawaka.

nalindi
walu

5

Walu, THE SUN

Moon and tides and sisters seven

It's early December and we're still sleeping outside; there aren't any mosquitoes and there's
no rain yet either. But there is the first lightning
and thunder, *wolma*. This lightning and thunder
is sending out messages to other countries
and other homelands, telling everyone – Yolŋu,
animals, plants – that the season of Barra'mirri
Mayaltha is coming. That's what you know as
'the wet season' – around December, January
and February. Are you listening? Are you looking,
smelling, feeling, tasting it? Quick, *Bäru*, this is
a message for you too, don't miss it. It's very
hot and humid during the day now, and we're
starting to sweat during the night.

The night sweating is a message telling us fruit like *larrani*, bush apple, is getting ripe.

When it's the hot time like this, *walu* (the sun) dries everything out, makes the leaves fall down. *Walu* dries the grass. *Walu* makes it very hot, tells us to sleep outside, makes us sweat. We might use our *raŋan* (paperbark) now as a cup, fold it over and use it to scoop up some water to drink and cool us down.

Walu tells us the time. Do you want to know the time? Look where *walu* is, look at the shadow, the shadow of the tree and the shadow of yourself. Or when it's about two or three o'clock you might hear a *garrukal* bird (kookaburra) singing, telling you the time, telling you it's nearly sunset. When the *garrukal* sings, the people remember that sunset is coming. This is the Dhuwa side of the story. *Wärrarra* is the Dhuwa sunset – *djäpana* is the Yirritja one. When *walu* sets it goes to the place where the people with yellow hair and light brown skin live; that's where *walu* goes at *wärrarra*.

Walu is very important and everyone loves it because it brings light and warmth. We use the word *walu* in many ways. When your washing is wet you put it on the *walu*, the clothesline, to dry; when you walk all the way from another homeland, you walk through *walupuy*, daytime. When you fish or get *ganguri* you always know there is *walu*, time. *Walu* tells you when to do these things. We use *walu* to measure things too. When we were little girls we'd use the *walu* at sunrise on *dharpa* (wood, tree) to measure ourselves. So *walu* is the sun, *walu* is the day, *walu* is time. *Walu* is very important for Yolŋu people; it is made by our ancestors.

Now, *walu* also tells us when it's time to burn the grass. It's the end of the burning time now. You drove down to Bawaka last night, didn't you, in the dark? Did you notice all those fires burning slowly through the undergrowth? They're beautiful, aren't they? Did you see the rows of flames all the way down the hills? Djawa set those fires you saw last night. He was driving into town to get you and he saw the dry grass. We're usually on our way somewhere, to do something, when we light fires. We love it when *dhimurru* blows because it means the rains are coming and you can burn everywhere. When it's burning time, you'll see fire wherever you go. Any time of day too.

We'll burn the grass around Bawaka as long as the wind is on our right as we come home. It depends on the breeze. If the breeze is coming from the east, we don't set fire to the grass, because we are worried the water tank might be destroyed. When there is a westerly wind, we can burn. When there is no wind and we want to burn, Djawundil will go and pour water around the water tank and the houses to protect them from the fire.

We burn for all different reasons. Sometimes we burn to clear up the grass, leaves and trees. We also burn to encourage fresh grass to grow for the animals, especially for the *dhum'thum* (wallabies). Fire is also useful for sending messages: if you are lost in the bush you can use fire to send a signal for someone to come and help.

There's so much knowledge to do with *walu*. There are songlines connecting it to Nature and the land; it is connected to people too. *Walirr* is another name for *walu* and it can also be the name of a person.

This *walu* is named by the Djan'kawu sisters, who came through here from Yaliŋbara. The sisters named everything. They named the sun – 'Let there be sun,' they said, and there was sun; 'Let there be morning star,' and there was the morning star.

All stories about *walu* are Dhuwa, and the *walu* songlines can be sung by Dhuwa people only, using sacred names.

Ooooh, did you hear that rumble? Quick, where is a pillow for me to put over my head? But we can stay out here for now. It won't start to rain just yet. In the next few weeks we'll start to get the afternoon storms and lightning, the clouds will start gathering in the west and at around three or four o'clock a storm will cool things down. But not quite yet. See that lightning over there? Lightning tells us stories. That one's a python snake – to a Yolŋu way of seeing, it's the tongue of the snake. It has many names in Yolŋu, same meaning but many names.

The lightning, the rains, the clouds, the winds and us, we're all connected, and all connected to *walu* too. *Bärra* is the rain that makes the sand soft. The grass gets long enough and the sand soft enough for *ganguri* to grow. *Bärra* helps grow big *ganguri*. And then the wind will turn and there'll be a new day when *dhimurru* wind knocks the grass over. *Bärra* is the name of the rain; it's also the name of a wind, and a season too. The *guya* get fat then and everybody loves it. And after that we get different rains again. Yirritja rain comes around July. It's a lighter rain than Dhuwa rain and comes in both Bärra and Dhimurru seasons. The rain and wind tell us when it's time for harvesting, on land and at sea, when all the fruits are ripe and the fish are plump.

When it's harvest time we sweat, because we are connected to the land and sea. For many months we still sweat at night because some fruit is ripening, maybe the white ones or maybe the red ones. Sweating is a message. It says the fruit is ripe. We are linked that way, you see. There are layers and layers and layers to our connection.

And the rains, clouds, winds, they're all a part of our songlines. There are songlines about the harvesting. Men sing people going out collecting fruits. And of course the clouds. In Midawarr you see the colourful clouds, along the sea horizon, and you know that's the time for harvesting.

People see them and know straight away that they should go and get *maypal* and *dhalimbu* (giant clam).

It's getting so hot now – oh that thunder! Drink some more *gapu* with your *raŋan* cup and make sure you come and sit in the shade here. I've told you about *walu* being Dhuwa, now let me tell you about Ŋalindi the moon. Ŋalindi is Yirritja. The moon is used to being born every month – a mother gave birth to the moon. When it's a new moon, it's a thin one and it shines away to people of different tribes. Merrki, why don't you tell the story about Ŋalindi and Lalu? This is another one of those bedtime stories we tell to our children, so they can learn all about *ŋalindi*.

A story about Ŋalindi and Lalu

MERRKI: OK, let me get comfortable, let me think. This is about Lalu the parrotfish, and Ŋalindi the moon. They were best friends. One day Lalu would come out and play with Ŋalindi, the next day Ŋalindi would go into the sea and play with Lalu. One day they had an argument about who lives above the sea and who lives below. So Lalu went into the corals and became part of the coral because of her colours. Ŋalindi was looking for her. 'Lalu, where are you? Lalu, Lalu, I am sorry. I still want to be your friend.'

But *bäyŋu*, nothing; Ŋalindi couldn't find her. Ŋalindi was sitting there crying because he couldn't see Lalu, and then Lalu came and said to Ŋalindi, 'Sorry, I'm going to live in the sea now.'

Ŋalindi was so angry with her. He said, 'If you do that you will go and you will die in the *gapu* now. But me, I will go up and I will live longer than you. When you die you die forever, but me, when I die I will come back to life again.'

Moons new and old

Aaah, that's better, that thunder is quiet now. Let me tell you more about *ŋalindi*. For Yolŋu people *ŋalindi* is hanging on a string and during the day *ŋalindi* goes into a big hole and stays there until it comes out again at night. *Ŋalindi* has lots of names. *Ŋalindi* means moon and *ŋalindi* also means month. *Wirripikili* is when *ŋalindi* is tiny, a new moon. And *walmuda* is a full moon. Ŋalindi lives by himself and he's got his own *djal dhuka*, his own path, going in and out; through the seasons, every day, his own path. Ŋalindi also has many layers too, like that *raŋan*; not one story, like Western understandings of the moon, but many paths.

Yolŋu know in which part of the month the moon dies, when only stars light the sky. There is 'nothing moon', *bäyŋu ŋalindi*, until a new moon comes. Last night, in the early morning, we saw a little moon, *wirripikili*. When the new moon comes, it's very important, it's like the beginning of a new month. We spread the news, calling 'New moon!' Sometimes there's also sorrow and we cry because Ŋalindi the new moon has come and it reminds us of our sadness for a loved one, maybe a sister who died in past months. Ŋalindi is a reminder. It has been a month since our loved one passed away. Or maybe we remember that next *ŋalindi* we have a tour group coming to visit.

Wirripikili sometimes brings lots of food. When we see a new moon, we welcome it. We make a *gurtha*, fire, and at twilight, everyone stands. Everyone must be quiet. We set a stick alight at the end. We hide the stick behind our back and go really quietly, stalking the moon. When we are close to a rock, we throw the stick at the rock. Grmm! Sparks fly everywhere. We call out, 'Let there be more *guya, ganguri, miyapunu.*' We only do this for the new moon.

At new moon, the tides will be really low and really high. The men might go night-fishing using their torches, looking for mullet and crayfish. Now the tide's going out, it's a good time for fishing, or getting *maypal* or *dhalimbu*.

When the moon gets big and full, that's *walmuḏa*, the tides move very quickly from low to high. *Walmuḏa* is very important for Yirritja people; there is a songline, a dance for *walmuḏa*. When they dance *walmuḏa* the dancers clap and lift their hands past their faces. *Walmuḏa* goes with the land, Nature, knowledge. *Walmuḏa* is a storyteller, he is a messenger, he tells us and all of Nature about the tides. *Walmuḏa* is also the best time for hunting and collecting foods. The men go out for *miyapunu*. When the tide is high the mud crabs come in and dig holes on the beach, so we don't look for them in the mangroves then, we look for their holes and dig down to get them.

So you see, the tides, *walu* and *ŋalindi*, Yolŋu, the land and Nature, we're all tied together. When it's full moon the tides only go halfway out and so we can't get some of our foods. We look at *ŋalindi* and see that we won't get *maypal* now because the tide won't go fully out. When the tide is low, that is the best time to spear crabs or collect *maypal*. We sit here under the *djomala* trees and as soon as we see *maypal* showing on the rocks down there we know the tide is going out and we quickly get in the car and head over to the other side, to the mangroves. The tides also tell us when to sleep during the day, when to take our naps. We sleep when the tide is high and it's no good for getting food.

We like the really big tides, the king tides, *bawuty* – they happen in cyclone season around late December, early January. They bring sand back to our *raŋi* (beach) at Bawaka. When we get a big cyclone it can wash the sand away and uncover the roots of the coconut palm trees along the *raŋi* – see over there how they're sticking up out of the sand? A big tide will help cover those roots again.

Ṇalindi sends a message to the tides and the people. Ṇalindi, the tides and us, we are talking with each other: *Walu* and *ŋalindi* carry messages to land, Nature, everything. And all these are messages for us, telling us something, like 'The *guya* are fat.' And the messages go in all directions. The call of the *gukguk* bird means the tide is coming in – even if you are 10 kilometres inland when you hear the call, you know the tide's coming in and so it's time for fishing. The *gukguk* is a type of pigeon. When you woke up this morning, did you hear it? *Guk-guk*, *guk-guk*, that's his call.

The animals are always looking for messages and sending them out too. When it's burning time and they see the grass on fire, the birds tell each other about it. They say, 'Let's find a safe place to stay where there's no fire.' For example, *garrtjambal* (red kangaroo) and *dhum'thum* (wallaby) run to the billabong for safety. One bird might fly over and tell the others and then they all spread the message too, telling about snakes, dingoes, goanna. They know the language. For thousands of years they've been doing this. We've learnt which animals to listen to.

Ah, it's cooling down a bit now. Let's move out from under the shade. Look at the clouds moving around, both Yirritja and Dhuwa clouds, mixing with each other. The wispy, soft, straight ones are our Dhuwa clouds. When we dance these clouds, we put *gara*, spears, on our heads. We use different sounds on our clapsticks to sing the different clouds in our songlines too. Those clouds now are making their sunset colours – they are message-carriers too, telling all of us, not just people but animals too, what to do, what the season is, when it's good for harvesting, when there's food. Do you remember the Dhuwa word for sunset and the Yirritja word for sunset – *wärrarra* and *djäpana*? But there are other Dhuwa and Yirritja names for sunsets too. See this *djäpana* now, remember it always. It's a beautiful sunset covering the water and land of Bawaka, sitting on us as we sit here looking at it. Yellow, orange, red, pink, it's showing us all the colours and showing us how beautiful life is, how good people are.

Look up, *walu* has gone to the place where the people with yellow hair and light skin live, and the stars are showing in our Bawaka sky. We've already started telling you about the stars – remember Banumbirr, the morning star? That Banumbirr is Djurrpun now. It is the evening star and it is Yirritja. We don't know where Djurrpun goes, but it disappears and when it comes back in the morning, then it's Banumbirr again and it's Dhuwa.

Now look, can you see the red glow from some of the fires burning around on the other side of the bay? Let's put some more wood on to keep warm. Yirritja and Dhuwa songlines tell us about fire, *gurtha*, and how and what to burn. You see the eye of the *gurtha* there, the deep red glow in the middle of the fire, that's *bäru* (crocodile) eye too – have you seen him looking at you at night? For Gumatj and other clans, *bäru* and *gurtha* are closely connected. But don't worry about that right now, we'll tell you about *bäru* later.

For now, lie back, look up at the stars and let me tell you a bedtime story. This is a campfire story, a story for children. It's a story we always tell women during the program that we run here for women visiting from down south. It's my dad's story and it's about the connections between the stars, *walu* and *gurtha*. This story explains how fire came to the land from the Seven Sisters.

The story of the Seven Sisters

You see, they're singing to *walu*, those Seven Sisters up there. That's why my mum, Gulumbu, makes stars – have you seen her paintings? They have been shown in the Museum of Contemporary Art in Sydney. If you carefully count the stars in her paintings, they are grouped, they are the Seven

Sisters. Well, those Seven Sisters came paddling all the way from Burralku, and they carried raw foods – raw fish, raw meat, *maypal* fresh off the rocks, in their canoe. Those Seven Sisters, they paddled all the way until they arrived on the land. And there was nowhere to get *gurtha*, so they started singing to *walu*, they sang, sang, sang, '*Walu*, give us *gurtha*'. They did this for maybe three or four days, singing for *walu* to drop them *gurtha*. The next day the sisters were weak, there was no food, and they couldn't eat raw meat. They were shouting, crying, 'Please, *walu*, give us *gurtha*.' A bit of *walu* broke off and fell to the land, an ember. So the sisters ran and got the *gurtha*, got the embers and put them in the grass and blew and blew until they became a *gurtha* and then they cooked *garrtjambal*, *maḏwija* (emu), *maypal*, *bäru*, *djinydjalma* (crab). They cooked and they ate. They ate until evening. *Walu* was going down and they wanted to rest.

Then all those animals they ate went up into the sky and turned into stars. And when you see the stars you can see all the animals' shapes. You can see the Seven Sisters sitting down. There, you look now. Can you see the shapes? Can you see the Seven Sisters, the *maypal*, *bäru*, and all the other creatures? They're always there.

Me, I've got two worlds.
I graduated with my studies at
college. And I graduated in my Yolŋu
world. Our stories are stories about
connections between all women. It doesn't
matter which colour, we're all the same.
Some women, when they hear this,
they cry. I love to work with them.

LAKLAK BURARRWANGA

Laklak's Story 5

KIDS LEARNING BOTH WAYS, YOLŊU AND ŊAPAKI

As the kids grew up, we had to do something about schooling. I didn't have the confidence to keep teaching them at Bawaka so we moved back to Yirrkala again. We stayed with my grandmother.

Djawundil, my eldest daughter, was a day student at Dhupuma College. Timmy and Aron, my two boys, were at Yirrkala school, and I was working there as an assistant teacher. My husband worked as a carpenter in and around Yirrkala. The other family members were still on the homeland at Guluruŋa.

When I first became a teacher I was nervous. I was so nervous! Bäpa told us, 'Be strong and study for the exams!'

While I was at the Yirrkala school, I worked with my sister and others on the bilingual curriculum. We wrote teaching resources in Yolŋu for the kids, to bring Yolŋu learning into the classroom. We wrote the story of *Bäru* the crocodile, and helped establish language workshops and excursions with Elders as part of the curriculum at the school.

We wanted the kids to learn both ways so that learning was an exchange between Yolŋu and *ŋapaki* knowledge. Knowledge doesn't just flow one way from ŋapaki to us. We have knowledge too. That's important for us and for our kids. At the school, we worked on making a *gänma* curriculum. *Gänma* is where the salt water and the fresh water meet and mingle, so there's a mixing. *Gänma* means new life, new ideas, knowledges coming together. It is where the two moieties meet and merge. Yirritja *gapu* and Dhuwa *gapu* come together at Bawaka, they mix and then go their own way. That's the power and that's the knowledge, with the *gapu* mixing. That's what we tried to do at the community school. That's what we're still trying to do.

We wanted to show how the world works, in our way of thinking. To us the rules of *gurrutu* (kinship – see chapter 7) are part of the patterns and cycles of the universe. For Yolŋu, there are logical orders in the land, there is counting and sharing (like in the *miyapunu* chapter), there is physics and measurement (as when we make *gara* for hunting), and there are cycles of growth and harvesting (which we've called 'natural farming' in chapter 8). We look at the water, at the tides coming and going, at the flows of the rivers and the movement of light through the sea and we see order and system there, almost like a form of maths. There is maths in the moon and the seasons, in the rain and the clouds. We know these things through the land. When a wind starts or a flower opens, that is the land teaching us.

During the time I'm describing I was studying to get my formal teaching qualifications. I was working half a day at the school and half a day studying with Batchelor College. I also used to fly around different homelands talking about starting schools. That was when Mandawuy Yunupiŋu was Principal. I was helping the homelands with teaching and planning.

I also spent some time with my father in Rorruwuy learning strong Datiwuy language, my clan language. When I was a child, I learnt Dhuwaya language from here, Yirrkala. But it is important that we keep our clan languages. The different clan languages are part of the diversity of the Yolŋu universe and were given to the clans by the Djan'kawu sisters. So going to learn my father's language was important to me.

djäparaḏuru
matha ŋanarr

6

Bäru, CROCODILE

Rain, tears, the eye of the fire

Let's sit down on the rocks and feel the rain. It's really soft during the day now in the short season of Barra'mirri. We can keep an eye on the kids playing in the water. Don't worry, it's safe. Nike the *bäru* doesn't come out until four or five in the afternoon, and during this time, around January and February, he is probably nesting anyway. Nike is a crocodile that we're closely connected to – Nike comes to visit us, eats fish off our beach, sometimes comes hunting with us. Nike is our mother and landowner.

We haven't seen Nike for a couple of months now, not since before Christmas, not since *wolma* the first thunder and lightning.

We know that *bäru* can hear the thunder. When we and the animals hear the first thunder, we all think, 'Ah that's the time, first thunder.' And so *bäru* know it's time for nesting. They mate first and then they go and work together to build their nests.

We wonder where Nike goes to build his nest. We do know what materials the *bäru* use. The *bäru* collect *raŋan*, *bewiya* (rushes that stand in the rivers), and *ŋulurr* (the long rushes). Male and female *bäru*, they both go and make the nest. Then afterwards they sit there all of December, January, February, through the really nice soft daytime rain until March, when the eggs hatch. If any birds, animals or people go to their nest to steal the eggs, those *bäru* get really angry.

In the olden times, when the old people wanted some eggs, they'd bang on the river to see if the male *bäru* was there. If the male *bäru* came up, they wouldn't touch the eggs because it would be too dangerous. You can tell a *bäru* is male because he is narrow. The female has a big belly. Then the babies hatch and the mother goes hunting and the father stays there, looking after the babies, teaching them to swim around the area of the nest. When the babies have learnt to swim and catch food for themselves, the female and male *bäru* leave them to find their own way.

My husband knew Nike as a baby. We feed him and he knows us. We talk to *bäru*, they talk back. They make moves with their head, and make sounds: *'Ack ack ack haaaaa.'* They talk, and we talk back by hitting the ground.

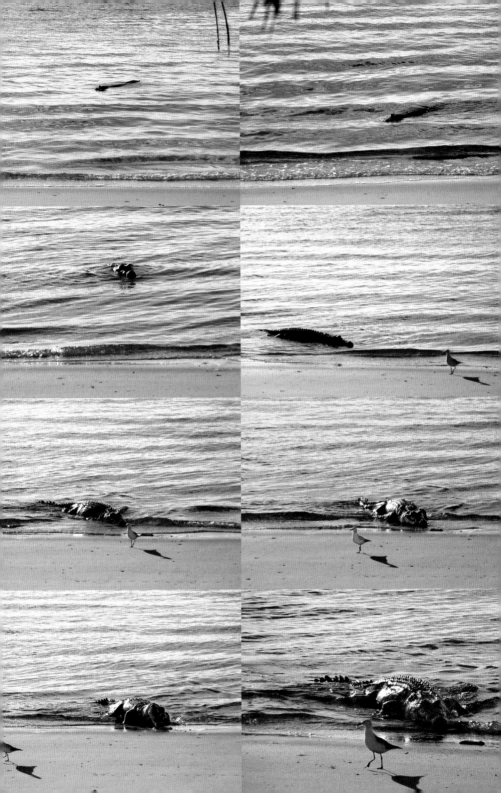

One time, Dhimurru, the local Indigenous land management organisation, wanted to come and catch this *bäru*, Nike, but we said no, he is part of our family, a protector of our land. Nike may be protecting this area and protecting us because of my husband's spirit. Sometimes animals can turn into humans, transforming from animal form to human form and back again, carrying story and song, and creating and passing on Law.

Nike sometimes comes hunting with us, following us to get some food. Sometimes we think Nike might have died. Then he comes around and splashes the water to tell us he's there. So he is part of our family. He's sacred.

Bäru is the foundational animal for my mother's country – both for Gumatj and Madarrpa people. Gumatj are of the *bäru*. They are saltwater crocodile people. *Bäru* are connected to the people of this land; they are in the paintings, in the dances and in the songs. Today, we're going to talk about how *bäru*, Country and language are all interconnected and why this is so important for us.

Both animals and people exist as part of Country – in fact, animals are co-creators of Country. Do you understand the concept of Country? Let me explain, because it's very important.

The meaning of Country

'Country' has many layers of meaning. It incorporates people, animals, plants, water and land. But Country is more than just people and things, it is also what connects them to each other and to multiple spiritual and symbolic realms. It relates to laws, custom, movement, song, knowledges, relationships, histories, presents, futures and spirits. Country can be talked to, it can be known, it can itself communicate, feel and take action. Country for us is alive with story, Law, power and kinship relations that join not only people to each other but link people, ancestors, place, animals, rocks, plants, stories and songs within land and sea. So you see, knowledge about Country is important because it's about how and where you fit in the world and how you connect to others and to place.

Listen to the *djilawurr* (bush turkey). They were out early this morning, calling to welcome you because you had been invited to Bawaka. Whenever there are tourists here who have been invited, the *djilawurr* sing. That's how we know you are welcome on this country.

In the same way that Country cares for us, we must care for Country. The well-being of all beings, of wind, water, sky and land, is related. The *djilawurr*, *lalu* (parrotfish), *miyapunu*, Bayini the spirit woman of Bawaka, water, wind and people are all interdependent.

When they come here, tourists always want to know how we mark the different ownership of land. There is no Yolŋu word for boundaries – instead we say *wäŋa*, place, homeland. We don't use signs for 'No Entry' or to identify boundaries, there is no sign for property. But that doesn't mean the land is empty or that there are no people who live on the land and care for it. You can go anywhere inland and see something that tells about the land – river, tree, rock. We are connected to the landscape, and that tells us the story.

Painting Country

We also use paintings to talk about where we belong, about Country. Painting is like writing or recording the story about your place. Our paintings are more than just colours or lines, they're about how we relate to each other, a social history, a ritual, an ancestral story and a personal history. A Yolŋu person can only paint something that belongs to

129

them and that they belong to. We use painting to tell the story from the beginning to the end. We can only paint about our own particular land, our particular sacred clan designs, our country.

Let's call the kids in, get them to sit down and have a drink, some food. That's better. Now Nanukala is looking at my drawing of the *bäru*, she is learning about where she belongs.

All the parts of the *bäru* have names, lots of names. Some names are sacred, and only men can say them. Different Gumatj people own different parts of *bäru* and so paint different patterns. We, the Burarrwangas and Bawaka, are the middle of the *bäru*. Look at the picture. We know straight away which Gumatj did the painting, which land they're from. If the painting is of *bäru* with the arms out, then it's by *Munuŋgurritj*, sea people, because *bäru* is swimming. If the arms are in, then *bäru* has stayed put and it's a Yunupiŋu and Burarrwanga painting. The paintings show a history of connections between different groups.

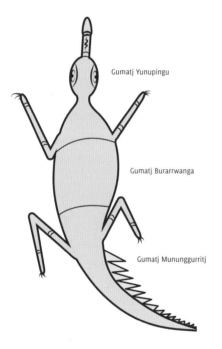

Gumatj Yunupingu

Gumatj Burarrwanga

Gumatj Mununggurritj

On a Gumatj painting of *bäru* are diamond shapes;

diamond patterns are our mother and grandmother, Guḻumbu's, pattern. She's Yirritja. The diamond patterns on the skin are significant, as they are mentioned in stories where *bäru* are thrown into fire and the marks are where the fire burned. We, the children from Gumatj, are the diamonds. The diamonds represent salt water and the power of the ancestral fire within. Gumatj have many stories about *bäru*, about its relationship to fire, the fierceness of the crocodile, about the female crocodile and birth and growth. One animal, lots of stories, lots of patterns.

Language makes us who we are

So *bäru* are connected to the Gumatj people of Bawaka. Three Gumatj groups meet around the area of Bawaka. If they need to talk about sacred business, they meet as one group. They sing, dance and paint *bäru*. They have Gumatj songs and Gumatj language.

Language is used in different ways and for different purposes: for culture, *Rom* (Law), songs, conversations and stories. We use different language for different levels: surface, middle and hidden. Hidden languages are not known to everyone and are used for specific occasions. Sometimes we use different words or a whole different language to speak to people in a certain relationship with us.

My mother and father spoke different languages. Our *matha ŋanarr*, our mother tongue (although remember we get our language through our father!), could be Dhuwa or Yirritja. The different Yolŋu languages have different moieties. For Yolŋu people, as we said earlier, a mother and father will always be of a different moiety. That means they will also have a different tongue. Children follow their father's tongue. So for mothers and daughters, there is a cycle. For women, Dhuwa speakers will be followed by Yirritja speakers and Yirritja by Dhuwa because a daughter is always the opposite moiety to her mother. You can't change your language, that's our Law.

All children at Yirrkala speak Dhuwaya and then they start learning their own – their father's language – when they're fourteen or fifteen. No child can change their language because who they are lives in the land. The young children learn about who they are as they learn how they relate to others and which language they use to speak to different people and groups. This helps their understanding of languages, lands and totems. Through language we learn about country, about boundaries, inside and outside knowledge. But even though we have different dialects, we learn the same way; we all have the same concepts. Everyone knows the time to get mud crabs or when to go collecting *ganguri*.

Language is your identity, who you are, where you come from. You always have your tongue and your tongue comes from the land. The language has been here for thousands of years and is still going on. If we lose our language we will be *bäyŋu*, nothing, we'll just be floating around. Language makes us strong. That's why we want it in schools.

Just as the paintings we told you about show the

boundaries between different clans, songs also show these differences. These songs talk about the relations between different things – winds, animals, blossoms, plants, foods, currents; they talk about who these things belong to, and how we relate to them. Men sing only their father's ancestral song. Women can cry through the songs of all their kin. If we see a dead *bäru* or women and *bäru* are giving birth and in pain, the women cry. All our mothers cry. Bawaka is a female country; when it's sunset, we women cry for joy and happiness.

The eye of the fire

Let's sit down by the fire. Look, it's *djäpana*. Call the kids in. They are tired from swimming all day. Look at all the pippies the kids have brought back with them. They dug them up by twisting their feet in the wet sand so the pippies rose to the top. Look, they are big ones. We can cook them on the fire. Get a pot so we can boil water, they will taste good.

See the red embers in the fire? At night-time *bäru* is the eye of the fire, of *gurtha*. So Gumatj people are connected by *bäru* to *gurtha*. There are 800 to 1000 songs and stories about *bäru*. Different clans have different stories. One Gumatj songline is about the rain and *bäru* together. The men of my mother's Gumatj clan, they sing about *bäru* getting all the *raŋan* and river rushes and waterlily leaves for the nest. Imagine sitting by the river, not too close, watching the mother *bäru* in labour. We would shed tears of joy. It would be amazing to see, it would be a lovely experience.

When Yolŋu women have a baby, they feel pain, and these mothers' pain is like *bäru*'s labour pain. The first day, the *bäru* mother thrashes around the nest, laying the eggs, while the husband watches. She lays lots of eggs, sometimes too many. She positions herself to channel the eggs the right way. This happens for both *bäru* and women; it happens during the lightning, the Yolŋu mother is crying and the baby comes out. The pain is the link. Women experience this, all women do the same, paining until the baby comes out. There is blood all over the nest when the *bäru* mother is resting; like women, the *bäru* sheds tears. We cry for the gift of the babies, and when we have lost our babies, just like the *bäru*.

After birth, just as for women, it's too soon for mother *bäru* to go out; she's too weak, she has to rest, she can't go hunting too soon. The husband goes hunting to get the food. As the mother *bäru* waits on the nest, the soft rain falls on *bäru*'s head, giving her knowledge and making a connection with Yolŋu people.

We have a songline about rain and connections between mother and birth, mother and child. I remember my mum crying, and singing a song about the *bäru* making fire and sending a message to the other Yirritja groups. There's a place at Birany Birany where the *bäru* lit the fire, where his nest was, and the flames got higher, then the sparks of the flames called Nilŋnilŋ floated away to another tribe, as far as the Arafura Swamp and the Gulf of Carpentaria.

Mat weaving tells how a
person is connected and where we
belong. The Yolŋu system of values and
beliefs is all tied up or connected like the
mat that is woven. We belong to the land, our
mother earth. We are one with it. The mat has
many stories, feelings and values that link the
Yolŋu woman. It is like the mother and child
relationship or the *yothu* and *yindi* connection
that is passed down through generations.
It is a story and knowledge that should
be told and given and maintained.

LAKLAK BURARRWANGA

Laklak's Story 6

MEMORIES OF MY MACASSAN FAMILY

In the 1980s, we decided to move as a family to Batchelor, south of Darwin, so I could finish my last year of teaching qualifications at Batchelor College. My husband and my boys Timmy and Aron all moved out there with me. Djawundil was still at high school, so she stayed in Yirrkala. I did my final year of study and Timmy and Aron went to school at Batchelor. It was hard. I was so homesick for family at home. Holidays were wonderful. We'd come back and see everyone, and find out how Dad (Bäpa) was going on. By that time, many people had come to Guluruŋa so Bäpa had three houses out there. The children loved the black-and-white TV at Guluruŋa.

When I was at Batchelor, I began to study Yolŋu connections with Indonesia and the Macassans. A lot of people think that before Captain Cook Australia was isolated from the rest of the world, but that isn't true. We had a long history of trade and connection with Asia, and especially with the Macassan people from Sulawesi in Indonesia. Yolŋu still talk about those days, and we've got lots of stories and songs about it. There are words and things we learnt from them too, like smoking tobacco from a pipe. Those connections, you know, were stopped by the Australian government. They made it illegal for those fishermen to visit us. Some families, those with people living over in Macassar, never saw their relatives again.

I heard a story about how one of my family's great-grandmothers had been taken from Arnhem Bay to Sulawesi when she was young. This was a long time ago. The Macassans were in Arnhem Land collecting trepang (sea cucumber) and this lady, Garŋarr, went with them. She grew up there, married a Macassan man, had children. While I was studying at Batchelor I started thinking of that woman.

I decided to study the story of Sulawesi and then I went. Six of us went to Sulawesi to trace the connection. That was a big adventure.

We stayed in Bali one night. The next day they heard on the radio that we were going to see that old lady, Garŋarr, our great-grandmother, and everyone was at Makassar airport waiting for us – all the Macassan sons, daughters, grandsons and granddaughters, and great-grandsons and great-grand-daughters and all the rest. They were lined up from the tarmac to the terminal. All of them were waiting for us. We were shaking hands and crying.

We got a special government car – me and my cousin – because we were from north-east Arnhem Land and they knew of the old people from there. First we went to the government hostel. It was very difficult for us because of the traditional living – the water, toilets and the restaurants – and because we didn't know the language.

The first two nights all the family came in, all the sons and their wives, to dress us up in traditional Macassan clothes to see the old lady. First we went to see the church to see where she used to sweep and mop floors, and the wood used in the building was ironwood from Arnhem Land. Then we moved to her village.

When she heard that we were from north-east Arnhem Land – they call us *Mariggi* people – she was crying. She jumped from the chair and walked towards us saying, 'This is the family from Arnhem Land.' She was still thinking of when she left many years before. So we grieved. She was crying for us and we were crying for her and we had a big dinner – a lot of people were there. It was a small house with lots of people and a big table. We had special traditional dinner – buffalo guts – and we were not allowed to spit it out, all the guides were there, we had to accept that food and drink the guts because it was their way...Oooh, hot one!

So we talked about what had happened to her. She told stories. She was really old – about ninety-nine – but she was very strong. She told the story for the great-great-grandsons. So we stayed there, kept her company. Her husband had now died. We stayed for one night with her, me and my cousin Djalinda.

The next day we went back and she called us up to say that we should go to the museum. Her nephew worked there. His name was Hussein. At the museum we saw all the things she used to wear, and her husband too. When she was young she was beautiful. He was a prince, her husband, and he had a sword. Everything was kept in the museum.

Afterwards, we had dinner with the other group of family – about a thousand people. I was sitting on an old lady's lap. She was feeding me. They treated me like a princess, because of my husband's name Baatjang (it means 'prince'). All the ladies they saying, 'Next time, you and your husband will come down.' People were touching me because I was black, asking me lots of questions. They thought I was from Africa and asked for Bob Marley. But I said I was from Arnhem Land, from *Mariggi*, that's Yolŋu. And they were crying for me that I didn't know them.

So they fed us, told stories, then afterwards we went to the parliament house and then the man at the government was talking about the *Mariggi* people, that we were the first people to open the door for Macassan people.

Then the next day we crossed in a Macassan boat to a small island and we saw the grave for the people from Sulawesi who had been to Arnhem Land. Their relatives took them to that island to get away from the city when they got old, and they died there. All the flags were there. It's similar to here.

One man took us to the wishing stone, a rock where they used to wish for the north-east wind. People on that small island, they'd cut the timber and made the boats. One really, really old man told a story about how they'd get ready. They'd wish for the north-east wind to come to take them to Arnhem Land. He talked about the wind and how many days it used to take to get across, then about old men, Aboriginal men, how they'd trade with trepang and which area.

Next day we drove in a bus to a cave to see the hands and the drawing of the Yolŋu people. They put their hands on the cave wall and drew some pictures – kangaroo, emu, echidna. To get to the cave we had to climb up about 300 metres, climbing, climbing right to the top. And when we got there we saw the hands of people who went there and the animals and the fingerprints of the Yolŋu. It was very special. There was a guard who kept an eye on the cave, a special guard with a gun.

Halfway back we had dinner and it was yucky frog leg with rice. We had seen the farm for frog-growing. We drove, really tired, got to the hostel, still there was no time to have a shower. We went to bed, we heard the call to prayer with the Imam; it was strange. It made me cry. We had to hide our arms, had to dress differently.

The next day all the family came in, and told us the old lady was getting sick. They brought us clothes, all the sons-in-law, cousins, sisters, they brought us different laplaps and other materials. And then we packed up. Everyone was at the airport to say goodbye to us and we flew back to Bali and to Darwin and to Batchelor. The next day we heard the bad news that the old woman had passed away. She died. We wrote a letter to the family. She was saying for a long time she wanted to see her Yolŋu family, tribal people, one time before she died.

I have the best memory of that, my first time overseas – seeing all the family, the island, meeting the people. The difficulties were the prayer through the speaker, and that some people talked English but some people didn't. Also the buffalo guts. The very, very best was when we went to a free disco! That's the last time I went to the disco. Good fun.

gurrutu
mälk

7

Gurrutu, KINSHIP

Layers of connection and belonging

There is a break in the rain. Let's take the mat out and sit under the tree enjoying the coolness. Will you rake the sand to get rid of the sticks and leaves that blew off the trees last night? With all these storms coming through, we get a lot of coconuts, fronds and other things on the beach. We need to rake them up each morning to keep things clean.

Thank you. Let's put this mat down and enjoy the chance to be outside. It's a time of big storms, this time of year, when it's Mayaltha, around February and March. There's a lot of lightning. Sometimes the winds bring a *warrk* or *motj* (cyclone) too. There's no cyclone now, so we are lucky.

There's not much hunting at this time of year, not with all this rain. In November and December we set some fires to clean and regenerate the country. Now in March there is much rain. Nature is growing all around us, ready for the next season, Midawarr, for harvest day. With all this rain, with all this growing, it's a good time to talk. Today we'll sit down and talk about kinship, about *gurrutu* and *mälk*.

Gurrutu and *mälk*, kinship and connection, are two of the things that underpin everything in a Yolŋu world. They are an extension of the moieties, Yirritja and Dhuwa, and the *yothu-yindi* (mother–child) relationship that we talked about at the beginning of the book. Remember, everything in the Yolŋu world is either Yirritja or Dhuwa and these two things give birth to each other – the Yirritja to the Dhuwa and the Dhuwa to the Yirritja – so that everything in the world is in a relationship of being both mother and child to all things. Well, *gurrutu* (kinship), and *mälk* (skin names), are the next layers in understanding. They provide the finer details of the pattern. If the broad outline of the pattern is given by Yirritja and Dhuwa and the *yothu-yindi* relationship, the intricate details, the richness of the design, is provided by the *gurrutu* and the *mälk*.

Gurrutu

Gurrutu is our pattern of kinship. Who is related to whom? Who is related to what and how? When we say 'related to', we mean who is your aunt, your cousin, your stepmother, but it is more than that too. These patterns of kinship cover all people *and* all things. It is an interlocking system that includes everyone and everything in relationship to each other. 'Who are you related to?' means 'How are you connected? How do you fit? Where are your ties, your obligations, where is your place in the world?'

We can name our relationship to thousands of people throughout Arnhem Land, and to plants, rocks and animals, spirits and celestial bodies, languages and land. It is a complicated system. To Yolŋu it is fundamental. It is something we are raised with, that is taught to us from birth. For *ŋapaki*, non-Indigenous people, it can be hard to follow. We'll talk a lot more about it today and we hope by the end you will begin to understand.

Our family members from down south are coming today: Sarah (Madirriny), Sandie (Ralapiny), and Kate (Ruwuk), with their children, Dawu, Raŋi, L̲alu, Gara, Miyapunu and Gal̲pu. They flew into Nhulunbuy last night and will drive out with Djawundil this morning. It will take them a few hours to drive across the sand dunes on the bumpy, sandy road. They need a four-wheel drive to get out here.

Let's have a cup of tea before they get here and talk some more. It is nice that the rain is holding off for a short time. The billy is on the fire. Here's the milk powder, the teabags and some sugar. Tea tastes better out at Bawaka, don't you think?

We can make a basket as we talk, too. See the way the pandanus weaves its way around? See the ways the colours merge and fit together? It's beautiful, isn't it? We thread each pandanus frond through the eye of this big needle. Here's a beautiful red colour for this part. We gather a small bundle of pandanus leaves and use a red piece to tie them together using this stitch, a blanket stitch. We go over and tuck it through itself. It makes a pattern. Like *gurrutu*. *Gurrutu* is what binds us together, what makes our underlying pattern of life. It gives meaning, it places us in the world.

Gurrutu is one big network of kinship and relationships. It is a web of life, life that goes from one person to another person to land to trees to rocks to water, wind, clouds, rivers, creeks, waterholes. The network of *gurrutu* makes a person who they are. It is what links a person to their land, to Nature and to other people. Everything fits and makes a whole. It's an everlasting web, and very strong. It's the core of Yolŋu culture, the essence.

Gurrutu is cyclical, like a helix, going up and around and up. For example, we have a *märi*, a grandmother. She has her *waku*, daughter, and her *gutharra*, granddaughter. Now the daughter of the granddaughter is not the *märi*'s great-granddaughter but rather her mother. See the pattern? The new-born baby is the mother of the old woman. The old woman is the new-born baby's daughter. If we draw it as a picture maybe it is easier to understand. We'll put in real people because it is a real thing.

So Laklak and Djawundil are *ŋändi* and *waku*, mother and daughter. L̲irrina is Djawundil's *waku* and Mawunymula is L̲irrina's *waku*. In a Western system, Mawunymula would be Laklak's great-granddaughter. But for Yolŋu she is her *ŋändi*, her mother. And Laklak is Mawunymula's *waku*, daughter,

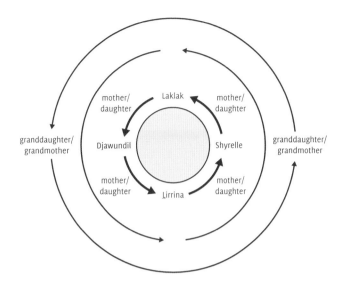

even though Mawunymula is just six years old. Rather than a line going in one direction from old to young, to us Yolŋu, it is a pattern, a circle that goes on and on. We have only put four people in this pattern so it doesn't become too complicated. But Laklak has mothers and grandmothers and daughters back in time too. And she has daughters and mothers and grandmothers still to come, as Mawunymula grows up and has children of her own.

And do you remember how a woman's children must have the opposite moiety to her – to keep that cycle of Yirritja and Dhuwa? To make sure this happens, if the grand-daughter comes through a male line (is a son's daughter), then we have different names and instead of the great-granddaughter being a mother, she will be an auntie.

Gurrutu is an infinite pattern. It goes on forever back-wards and forever forwards. It doesn't matter how old you are, you are connected and a relative to someone else, to everyone else. Even if a baby is not there yet, we know who they are related to, who is their mother, their daughter, their aunties and grandchildren. That is *gurrutu*.

Wait, is that a troopie coming? Can you hear that? It must be Djawundil with Kate, Sandie, Sarah and the kids. Ah, here they are!

'Welcome back. It is so good to see you. We have missed you and look how the kids have all grown!'

This is our adopted family. Kate, Sandie and Sarah are from Macquarie and Newcastle universities. We have been working together for five years now. Our lives have become intertwined. Each year, these three and their families come up to Bawaka. We write things together, we share knowledge, we talk and the children play. We talk together, work together, so we can understand each other. Indigenous and non-Indigenous make a unity and friendship for the future.

Giving names and adopting Kate, Sarah and Sandie and their families into our family has been a way of giving back. It's very special. They and all their family members will always be a part of our family now. Their children and parents, they will always belong here. When they are old, they can come and visit their family in Arnhem Land.

When we go away from Bawaka, we take our children and grandchildren too. We all went down to Sydney and Newcastle for a book launch, an exhibition and some workshops. We stayed with Kate, Sandie and Sarah down there. Taking our kids was important. Nanukala made lots of friends, playing and exchanging culture. Sometimes when Kate, Sandie and Sarah leave, we cry, we miss them.

We think about them when they are gone, we talk about them. We're always thinking about family.

When we went south for the book launch, Banbapuy's granddaughter Bangaditjan (Dharrpawuy) adopted Sarah as her big sister. Sarah's husband Matt was then adopted in with the correct *mälk* and *gurrutu* that would make him a good husband for Sarah. Sandie was adopted as Laklak's sister, and Kate as her daughter (and Djawundil's sister). We knew this is how it should be. We gave them all names too, and their children. Many people who work with Yolŋu are adopted into a family so that they too will have a place within the universe, like other Yolŋu, like the land and birds and trees.

Look, here comes the rain! Quick, rush, gather the mats and weaving, scoop up the kids and run indoors. Leave your things in the troopie for now.

When the rain comes, it really comes. Look at the water turn grey and the blur of the horizon that shows the rain on the way. We can see it as it comes across the water. Then we feel it, first the wind, then the rain coming down strong.

We'll spread the mat out on the floor at the edge of the kitchen. It is open on the side so we can see outside but we'll be out of the rain. We can catch up together a little.

Djawundil bounces Galpu up and down in her lap. '*Waku, waku*,' she says. She is repeating his relationship to her. That's what we do.

When a child is born we say '*Manyi, manyi*' (Grandmother, Grandmother) or '*Gäthu, gäthu*' (Niece, Niece) to them. We are telling them what our *gurrutu* is to them, what our

149

relationship is, so they grow up knowing this person is their *manyi* or their *gäthu*, even before they know the person's name. They start by saying the *gurrutu* name, then they learn the other names.

Our little ones, like Nanukala, Mawunymula and Siena, are already figuring it out. They know who they are and how other people relate to them. They know how they relate to other things too, to plants and animals, to winds and waters, to celestial beings, languages and countries. We are always reinforcing this knowledge. It helps them behave well. They know what is right and wrong between them and other people and things.

We have been talking about people, but there is the land, the animals. They all have *gurrutu*.

A child says, 'Look at that rock.' We answer, 'Oh yes, that is your *märi*, your grandmother.'

Siena might say, 'Look at that whale.' We answer, 'That is your *yapa*, your sister.' It is Djawundil's *yapa* too and Arien's and Djawa's and Ruwuk's. Siena is now nine, and when anything to do with whales happens, she says, 'That is my *yapa*, my sister.'

Gurrutu links all things in a way that lasts forever. In our Country, there is some mining. We didn't want the mining on our land but it happened, even though we said, 'No, that mining is not right.' Now, many trees and some country have been removed. Those trees aren't there any more but we still sing them, we still keep them alive, remembering them. They are still linked through the web of connections. Their *gurrutu* still holds them.

Gurrutu is in our art too. Perhaps you have admired the patterns, the symmetry and the beautiful images you see in Aboriginal art? Perhaps you have wondered what it means? Of course, there is a lot of Aboriginal art from many different Aboriginal cultures over Australia. For Yolŋu, the art is linked to *gurrutu*. It is another way that we represent our kinship with the world.

Look at the picture on this page. My mother (also Ritjilili, Merrki and Banbapuy's mother, of course) painted that picture. She was a famous artist. It is a picture of a mother quail, who is Yirritja, and her babies. It is the story of *yothu-yindi*, the mother–child relationship. This is *gurrutu* too. It is a cycle going to infinity. We all fit in this cycle.

In the baskets we are making, there is the story of *gurrutu*. The story is there in the connections, in the colours and the patterns. It is in the way it all comes together. Everything is included, as in a basket woven from many colours. Everything cycles outwards in an infinite pattern. The rules of *gurrutu* underpin our life. *Gurrutu* is the world.

Poison relationships

Gurrutu is a guide about what is right and what is not right. It tells us who could be acceptable as a marriage partner and who could be our best friend, but it also tells us who we *cannot* marry, who we should avoid. We have already mentioned that you cannot marry someone of the same moiety. That is a fundamental rule for us. Dhuwa cannot marry Dhuwa, Yirritja can't marry Yirritja.

There are other avoidance relationships. For example, we have a *mukul rumuru*, which is sometimes called a 'poison auntie'. The relationship between boys and their poison auntie is especially important. A poison aunt is a boy's mother's mother's brother's girl-child, and he avoids contact with her but gives her deep respect. The brothers of those poison aunties, they are the best mates of that boy. A best mate is one you can pour your heart out to, tell all your secrets; you joke together and laugh. He is called *maralkur* or *gala*.

Another poison relationship is with your mother-in-law. For a man, like Rrawun, this is your wife's mother or the mother of your brother's wife. This is also someone that you avoid all contact with. You can't talk directly to them and you shouldn't sit next to them. You can't use their name. I think there are many non-Indigenous men in Australia who wish they could have this avoidance relationship with their mother-in-law!

These are just two avoidance relationships. We have others. After initiation, brothers and sisters avoid direct contact with each other. Even if a child is not born yet, we still know where they fit. We know who is a potential wife or husband, and who is in a poison relationship. The story we'll tell at the end of today is about a *ŋathiwalkur* – a girl's mother's mother's brother's wife's brother – called Bamapama. It is a warning story.

We've put a game in (see below) to see if you understand *gurrutu*. It's about a plane ride and how you decide who you sit next to. The way you have to sit in a plane or a car, the relationships you have with other people, the names we give our children, these are all ways this big and beautiful pattern is experienced day to day. It is not just a story for us, and not just something from the past. It is now, the present, and the future.

A *gurrutu* puzzle, invented by Merrki

There are five Yolŋu travelling together on the plane from Nhulunbuy to Darwin. On one side of the aisle there is a group of three seats. On the other side there are two seats. The five Yolŋu must decide how to arrange themselves. There are

two brothers, Djawa and Rrawun
a sister, Djawundil
the wife of one of the brothers, Yalmay
and the wife's mother, Marrpalawi

Try to decide where everyone must sit. You will have to ignore the boarding passes to keep to the rules of *gurrutu*. The answer is given below.

ANSWER: brother brother wife AISLE sister mother-in-law (The brothers cannot sit close to the sister or especially the mother-in-law, but the wife can talk to anyone.)

Mälk

Mälk is the other underlying pattern that goes along with *gurrutu* to define how we all fit together in our own community. All Yolŋu, and Indigenous people all over Australia, have the concept of *mälk*. It is sometimes called 'skin name'. *Mälk* is another way of knowing your place, knowing where you fit. You get your *mälk* from your mother, almost like a surname. You don't have the same name as your mother but your mother's place in the cycle of *mälk* determines your place in a set order. Yolŋu have a set of sixteen *mälk*, or skin names. There are eight Dhuwa and eight Yirritja, four of each for men and four for women. Everyone has one of these names. That means *mälk* is like a passport. By someone's *mälk*, you know where they fit in relation to you.

For example, a woman who is *banaditjan* has a baby girl who is *galiyan*, *galiyan* has *gutjan*, *gutjan* has *bilinydjan*, *bilinydjan* has *baŋaditjan* and the cycle begins again. So if we look at my line, I am *galiyan*, so my daughter Djawundil will be *gutjan* and her sons, Djawa and Aron, will be *gutjuk* (boys have a male version, girls a female version, but it is still the same skin name). Djawundil's daughter Lirrina is *bilinydjan* and Lirrina's daughter Mawunymula is *baŋaditjan*. Now we have completed one cycle. If Mawunymula has a daughter she will be *galiyan*, just like me. It fits with the *gurrutu* here. Remember we said before that Mawunymula is my little mother. Now you can see her daughter will be the same skin as me. It all fits together.

155

There is another sequence for women – the sequence of *ŋarritjan–gamanydjan–buḻanydjan–wamuttjan*. A woman of the *mälk ŋarritjan* has a daughter *gamanydjan*, a grand-daughter *buḻanydjan* and a mother/great-granddaughter *wamuttjan*.

If any of the girls have a boy, then the boy's *mälk* becomes part of another sequence. The boy's *mälk* is determined by his mother but his children's *mälk* will be determined by *their* mother.

Let's look at my son Djawa. Djawa is *gutjuk*. He has had children with three women. His first wife was *gamanydjan*. He has one daughter, Marcia, with her; Marcia is *buḻanydjan*. His next two wives were both *wamuttjan*. With them he had two girls, Nayari and Bayini who are both *narritjan*, and three boys, Bowi, Dhimathaya and Djerra, who are *narritj*. So Djawa's children, because they have different mothers, have different *mälk*, different passports.

Mälk is your identity. When you visit a community you haven't been to before, you tell people your *mälk* and people know who you are and then they can match you up to the *gurrutu* system. 'Ah,' they might say, 'you are my *yapa*, sister,' or 'my *mukul*, aunt,' or 'my grandmother, *märi*.' So *mälk* is important to Yolŋu people all over. It is another way of fitting into the pattern.

All through north-east Arnhem Land, we look for *gurrutu* and *mälk*. Say if Dawu grows up and comes back to visit some day and says, 'I was adopted when I was a baby. My mother was here a long time ago. I am *galiyan*.' Then the person she's speaking to can say, 'Ohhh, you are my mother or my sister, come in!' Dawu would be introduced to the others through her relationship with them. That is how you work out where you fit in.

That is enough for now. I hope you have begun to understand. It is a long conversation about *gurrutu* and *mälk*. It is complicated. In a Yolŋu world, it is something we are born with. We are always talking about it. When we have babies, we don't call them by their given name, we call them by their *gurrutu* or their *mälk*. '*Waku*', we might call them, or '*Banaditjan*'. So they learn who they are right from the

start. Only when they are two or three years old do we begin to call a baby by its given name. That is why we know *mälk* and *gurrutu* so deeply. It is the first thing we hear.

Raŋan, the paperbark tree, can help us understand the layers and how the *mälk* and *gurrutu* wraps around and around, spiralling to infinity. That is kinship. That is connection.

Now it is *djäpana*. We'll finish today by telling you a story about *gurrutu*. The story is not a happy one. *Gurrutu* binds us together, it helps us know our place, but it also tells us what not to do. It tells us things can go wrong if

157

we do not behave. This is the story of Bamapama and it is especially for girls.

We were told this story when we were young. You know why? So that we would be aware of strangers, and know about avoidance relationships. It's a warning.

Bamapama: a warning story

There was a Yolŋu camp. A family was living there, a clan. One day a man arrived from another clan. This was Bamapama. He was her *ŋathiwalkur*, grandmother's brother's wife's brother to one of the girls living there. This is an avoidance relationship. He had been at a ceremony with the girl's parents, a long way away, and he brought a message from them.

'I need to get the dillybags with all the food and things and take them back for the ceremony,' Bamapama said. 'But it is a long way away so I need a young girl who is really fast and strong to carry them there.' Then he said, 'Girls, show me how fast you can run.'

He announced a contest for all the young girls in the camp. The girls would have to run and jump as high as they could. So the next day all the girls lined up. The first one ran, ran and jumped. He said, 'Oh that was good, but not as high as I'd like.'

The next one came to run and jump.

'That was good but not high enough,' he said again. And so it went on for the next girl and the next. The one girl who was in an avoidance relationship to him hadn't had her turn yet. Because of this relationship, he couldn't speak to her, but he watched her all the time.

At last this young girl ran and jumped.

He said, 'Yo, yo! You are the one who will take the things.'

The whole camp clapped.

He declared, 'This is the one who will come with me because she jumped the highest.' Really, she just jumped the same as the others.

Remember, Bamapama was the girl's *ŋathiwalkur*.

The next day, they packed up food and everything. He put it all in a *bathi*, a basket, the one that goes around the forehead and right down the back. He gave it to the girl to carry as well as a *bathi* for each shoulder. He just carried the spear and the spear-thrower, the *gara* and the *galpu*. The whole camp said goodbye to them.

They walked for a long, long time. They walked all day. When evening came, they set up camp. Bamapama made two shelters, one for her and one for himself. Then he said, 'I know a little billabong where we can catch fish to eat for dinner.'

The purpose of going to the billabong was to make himself known by his penis.

So they went to this lagoon, and saw the water churning with crayfish. They jumped in, they waded with their hands outstretched for *ganngal*, catfish, and *djaykung*, filesnake. At each end of the lagoon they felt for these creatures, and for eels, and caught them and threw them onto the bank. Feeling, feeling, the young girl tried to catch what she felt but each time it would escape. She could feel it but couldn't quite catch it. It was Bamapama's penis.

In the end they said, 'We've got everything. Let's go back and make a fire and eat our dinner.'

They cooked the eels, the *ganngal* and filesnake. They ate and it was time to go to bed. The young girl said, 'I'm going to go to sleep.'

He said, 'I'll stay here and watch a little and then go to sleep too.'

During the night, the girl heard crying. '*Wa wa wa!*' Bamapama called, 'Come and help me.'

Bamapama had put blood from the catfish on his foot and now pretended that he had cut himself. The girl rushed in, saying, 'What is wrong?'

'I cut myself.'

The young girl got *raŋan*, paperbark, and some reeds to clean his foot. He said, 'I'm dying, I'm bleeding, help me.'

The young girl cleaned it up. Then she used reeds from the lagoon as a dressing and wrapped the foot up with paperbark.

He raped that young girl.

The next morning the young girl came limping back to the ceremony where her parents were. Her parents saw her coming, limping, all sodden, ashen-faced, crying.

'What is the matter with you, my daughter?'

She told them, 'That man did a bad thing to me.'

'*Wa, wa!*'

Men brought out their spears. 'We are going to kill you, Bamapama!'

160

Bamapama did a dance and started singing, 'Are you like that? I am more fierce!'

When the fathers and the uncles got the spears to kill him, they were doing the dance of the kill. He says, 'Oh you're like that, then. Let me show you I can do that too.' And he started spearing and instead of spearing any of them he speared the dog. That means he was a coward. He was telling himself, 'I can rape a young girl but I can't spear a person, only a dog.'

So they speared him and he was killed. In the end it was the girl's father who killed him.

The moral of the story is to never be a Bamapama. That is why we call someone who is stupid but pretending to be brave, someone who is cocky, 'Bamapama'.

There is a moral for young girls too. You might think you know that old man, but you don't really know him. You must follow the rules of *gurrutu*, or bad things can happen.

Every story we tell has a moral that we need to follow. When children grow up hearing those stories, they start to realise that this is the Law.

Sign language

There is a sign language for *gurrutu*.

You sign the **backbone** and that is the grandmother
(the mother's mother, or *märi*) – because they are
the backbone. So Merrki is the backbone of Galpu
and Lirrina. She is their *märi*. She is their strength.
She will stand up and walk tall for them.

The **forehead** is the paternal grandfather,
the father's father, or *mamu*. This is everything
to do with knowledge.

The **chin** is the father's father or the father's mother.
This is your *ŋathi* or your *momu*, wisdom.
When men grow older, when they reach 50 or 60
or more, they might grow a beard, maybe decorate
the beard with feathers. It shows they have wisdom.

The **breast**, usually right side, is the mother.

The **stomach** is a baby.

The **hips** and **upper leg** are husband or wife,
because you have to be close to each other.

The **lower leg** is a brother or sister.

The **shoulder** is aunt or father.

The **wrist** is uncle.

The **knee** is *gurrung*, the poison relationship
of son-in-law or daughter-in-law.

The **elbow** is an avoidance relationship.
You point at the elbow or touch it.

BACK TO BAWAKA

So I finished my teaching diploma and we moved back to Yirrkala. I worked in Yirrkala School, maybe three or four years. But then my husband started getting sick. This was in the 1990s. At that time Djawa (Timmy) was working as a builder. He was still single. Aron was at high school in Nhulunbuy. He finished Year 12 and went straight to his first job, as a ranger with the land-management organisation, Dhimurru.

Djawundil finished college and got a job with the Yirrkala Dhanbul Association, like the local council. She was working at reception and as a payroll clerk and creditor clerk. Djawundil had kids, then separated from her ex. Timmy had his first son, Bowi. So I had Bowi as first grandson. I had him from one year old. I bottle-fed him, grew him up.

At Bawaka, an old man passed away, lost at sea. For two years Bawaka was off limits – we needed to leave it alone. My husband Baatjang was sick during that time, so it was really hard. He had that sickness really strong.

One day, we flew out to Barrkira for a weekend holiday. We had a talk with key members of my family, Auntie Djawundil and Dtaŋadtaŋa, and we sat down and wrote a letter to Laynhapuy Homeland Association saying that we wanted to move back and establish Bawaka again. When we got back from Barrkira we went straight to Laynhapuy and our request went to the board. One of the Elders, Dhungalla, he was the caretaker for Bawaka, and he agreed. Bawaka is Country for my husband. So they said 'yes', because of the sickness; my husband didn't want to die in Yirrkala, he wanted to go back to his homeland. I had my grandson Bowi, just a baby, and my husband, and we moved. Other family followed us.

And then I worried. I was thinking, 'What will I do at Bawaka? There is no job.' I was used to teaching at the Yirrkala School. No job, and during the wet season how would I cope? But I am lucky that my mum taught me how to hunt according to the seasons, how to grow gardens, wash clothes and look after the house. So I did.

And I thought, 'I might have a school.' So I started a school with my grandchildren. There were about ten of them, including Bowi. Three or four children came across the bay from Dhaniya too, each day.

I started the kids writing on the sand with fingers. We had no paper, no pencil, and that is really, really hard. We were handwriting in the sand, and counting shells and sticks and learning with the tides. It is in the curriculum, we look at the tide lines. And we were counting the islands and counting the houses or taps. The kids learned simple English – 'My name is So-and-so', 'Hello, how are you?', or 'Good morning'.

We used one small room, or sat on the beach for classes. And the children thought it was funny, the bush school. One day my grandson Damybawe came around, and he heard the name of the school and he said, 'Which school? Yirrkala School?' and I said, 'No, a new school, we have opened a homeland school.' And he began laughing, 'I can't believe you have school here!' It was a room of the house, with all the blankets on one side!

And they said, 'Where can we sleep, in this school?' and I told them, 'Anywhere!' It is very different.

Rrawun was one of my students. He's my youngest sister Banbapuy's son. He had a real vision. He always loved to sing, drum and play guitar. I'd buy him a little guitar for best attendance. He loved to write songs. Timmy, Aron and Rrawun would sit and write songs about Bawaka. The first song they wrote together is called *Dhutarra* (woman). I was involved and so was my husband, helping with the words, spelling in English. Rrawun finished his school there. He did Years 11 and 12 by correspondence, with me helping him through. He's successful now, with a band called East Journey. They've got an album, and that first song is on it.

I raised Bowi there and Rrawun and my other grandchildren, like Nanukala and Gapirri. I bottle-fed them all. Brought them all up.

It was hard at home in those days. We drank the *gapu* (water) from the tank. And in the wet season there was no sun, *baaynu walu*, and during the dry season only a little bit of *gapu*. So we usually had only one day for washing all the clothes, then we'd stop for four or five days until there was plenty of water again. We used to have a generator for lights from seven until eleven o'clock and everyone went to bed until morning. Now we have solar.

And we had *baaynu natha* (no food), tea or sugar, during the wet season because it rained all the time and you can't drive out when the land around the creek is covered with water. No helicopter, no boat. We were stuck there but we tried hard, going out fishing and getting yams and drinking

water. Sometimes we had no sugar so we had to have tea with syrup or honey. That reminded me of the old days when I was a young girl. Syrup with tea, and honey with tea! I told stories about the long time ago to my grandsons and granddaughters. Sometimes we sit around and laugh and tell stories.

It was the late 1990s by this time. Timmy had a baby girl, Bayini Burarrwanga. He was still single. Rita was the mum, and Rita's father came and talked to me and my husband. He wanted Timmy to go to Darwin to marry Rita. So we sent our son to Darwin for maybe two years. He got married. We were there at Bawaka, by ourselves. Then one day, Timmy came with his third baby, Theo. He came with Rita to Bawaka in the troopie. They didn't ring us, just came as a surprise, driving all the way from Darwin!

While Aron was studying to be a ranger at Batchelor, he met Atilya. In two years he finished school and brought Atilya to meet us at Bawaka. We gave permission for Aron to marry Atilya and they moved to Yirrkala, to the green house. In 1999, their first son, Jerry Gapirri, was born. My husband was very, very happy. Our grandchildren were brought up here at Bawaka.

In 1999 my husband was getting worse and worse. His poor health was a real problem. I was on the radio calling 'Echo, Tango, Victor, Mike' from Bawaka. It was very hard for me, running around, calling the hospital, calling family. There were no people, no car, just a little radio. Sometimes family from the other side of the bay, from Dhaniya, would come and help. It was about that time that the radio finished and we got the public phone out here. Our kids were away by then, some at work, some still at school. We were suffering at Bawaka.

And then my husband died. When he died, he came back to Bawaka, to Yirritja country because he was a Yirritja man. But he is also connected to Dhuwa country and Dhuwa people. On his knowledge, he's holding two lands, Bawaka (mother) and land on other side (child). This is *yothu-yindi*. Your home is where your bones go when you die. When you die you go back to the soil, where you came from.

My husband and the old people are always here, present with us. When someone dies their bones go back to their homeland – their own soil, their own *gapu*. The Yolŋu word for homeland is *wäŋa ŋaraka*. *Wäŋa* means land and *ŋaraka* means bones.

Standing by my husband's grave at Bawaka is the mast of a Macassan boat, it's his knowledge pole. It's a memorial pole for him, his spiritual foundation. His knowledge has been given to our family. His wish and hope is in me, a mother, to take care of this land and his children while he's buried here. And his dream is still alive, passing through the generations.

ganguri
gay'wu
gukguk

8

Ganguri, YAM

Bush foods and natural farming

Is that *gukguk* calling? When we hear *gukguk* calling us, here at Bawaka, we know it's time to go digging for *ganguri,* yams. It's Midawarr, April this year. Midawarr is the ideal season for gathering yams – after the heavy rains have ceased at the end of the wet season, and before the proper dry season. *Gukguk* is telling us to remember to take water because it's hot, hard work digging *ganguri.* So let's get our *wapitj* (digging stick) or *baki ki* (wire) and our dillybag, and call the children.

Make sure you cover up the babies, there are lots of flies and mosquitoes around. The flies are the owners of the earth during Midawarr, they're everywhere. They're sending out the message that the stingray are ready to eat now, and that there are lots of fat fish too, small and big. The crabs are soft now too, small but with lots of meat. You can keep eating those crabs until the gum tree has the orange flowers – yes, the one you see at Garma Festival time, in August. Then the crabs grow big and have eggs. This time of year the north-east winds blow, the sea is calm and it's a good time to hunt *miyapunu* and *djunuŋguyaŋu* and to harvest *dhalimbu* (clam). During Midawarr the plants grow and the animals are fat. It is my favourite season. Every day is harvest day.

Now is the time to get all the *ŋatha*, the food that women collect. We want you to come with us and collect *ganguri* so you can see how we teach the children, how they learn about different foods, measurement and other things. This is the women's job, although men can come digging *ganguri* too if they want.

'Nanukala, Mawunymula, Raŋi, Lalu, Gara, Miyapunu, Galpu and Dawu, come on, let's go.' The children always come along, it's the way they learn to hunt and collect food. It's the way we learnt too; the grandmothers and the mothers, aunties and sisters all teach the children about how to identify different foods and vegetables from the bush. Today we have the troopie, so let's all climb in and we can drive over to get the *ganguri*.

When we go collecting *ganguri* we always gather as we go. The children pick fruits, like *larrani* (bush apples)

and *djunpu* (figs). We can also get some *butjiriŋaniŋ*, bush medicine; we use it for the skin, it's good if you are itchy or have skin problems. *Nambarra* is good for the flu. We are always collecting, that's what Yolŋu ladies are like. We go for one thing and come back with lots of different things. As we walk, we collect, we hunt and we learn what we can get during the Midawarr season.

Yolŋu bush foods

MURNYAN (plant or vegetable food)

Borum fruits
Guku bee products
Natha root foods
Manutji natha seeds
Mudhunay cycad foodstuffs, e.g. cycad 'bread'

GONYIL (meat, shellfish, eggs)

Warrakan land animals and birds
Miyapunu marine mammals, or turtle
Maranydjalk rays and sharks
Guya fish
Maypal shellfish, crabs
Mapu eggs

Here we are, let's get out. Make sure you keep an eye out for snakes, spiders and paper wasps.

Look, Nanukala is crying. What's wrong? 'Oh it's the ants, they're biting your arm. Here, let's swipe them off.'

It is okay. It is important for her to know the ants and for the ants to know her. It's by living in Nature that we build and understand our rich relationships with the animals, the seasons and with each other.

Ah, here is a good spot, let's put the *wapitja* into the sand to see if it is soft enough.

Yes, that's good, nice and soft, and look, you can see some *ganguri* vines and leaves. The leaves of the *ganguri* tell us a lot about the condition of the underground parts of the plant. See there, the leaves are big and heart-shaped. That's a good *ganguri*. It has a really big string, a big vine. So we know it's a really good one to dig up. During Midawarr the ground is not too wet and therefore the yams are not soggy or waterlogged. They are also at their most nutritious in Midawarr, loaded with starch. Later in the season they get hard and don't taste very good. This vegetation is very different from the dry season when the leaves are very dry and we set fire to the bush and burn the grass as well as the leaves and vines of the *ganguri*.

There are plenty of different yam species, some Dhuwa and some Yirritja. Some can be eaten raw, others need elaborate preparation. We know from the old people which ones to eat and which ones are just for the kids to play with. There are also the new ones from this year, which we eat, and the old ones from last year, which we leave.

When we find one, we call out to the other women, 'We got *ganguri* here, you can go and look for more *ganguri* but we have to dig this first.'

Let's sit down and follow this vine, look carefully for snakes, spiders and ants first. We'll start digging using the point of the *wapitja*. We can also use our hands and arms.

One person starts digging but they'll need to rest. Someone else then has a go. We take turns because getting the sand out and digging a deep hole is hard work. One person keeps going until they reach the depth of their arm, then you get someone with a longer arm – we usually take Sasha, Djawundil's daughter, with us because she's got such long arms!

Now the hole is deeper, you need to lie on your belly and dig. Then sit in the hole and keep digging. You find the vine at the top and keep following it down, very, very carefully clearing around it so you don't break it. See, we followed this one all the way down and here is the top of the yam tuber. Keep digging. There, we got it, see, it's a good one. Put it in the dillybag with the others.

Women are natural farmers. The foods have their own cycle of living and growing. We don't water them, they don't need us to water them. They have their own knowledge and they can grow by themselves. When we come back next year, *ganguri* is still there. The rain carries the sand back to cover the *ganguri* again.

We usually keep digging until we have enough *ganguri* to feed the family and to share. We don't pull everything out or take it all. We just carefully go and get what we want. If we hadn't driven here, we'd have to limit our takings anyway. We must bear in mind how long the journey home is, and how much we can carry. The children will help carry the yams, wood, fruit and other things we have collected, but it's much easier when we have the troopie.

We have enough now, let's gather our things. Make sure you drink some water; it's very hot. See, all the children are good at helping, they are working together to bring home all the things we have collected.

It is very important for us to walk through the land, to walk together, to see Nature grow by itself, to know there is food for us, waiting. We don't ask someone is the food ready? No, we can see for ourselves, through the cycle of the seasons, the knowledge that has been there for thousands of years. We don't read it in a book or paper. We read it every day, every minute, every moment. We share that knowledge with the children, and now with you, it's a part of us.

It's been a long drive back. Let's sit down and we will show you how we cook the *ganguri*. First we make a big fire and when it's burnt to ashes we take all the sticks out but leave the hot stones, dig into the hot sand and bury the *ganguri*. We also put in special wet grass from the lagoon and then cover it with *raŋan* – this makes steam that cooks the *ganguri*. We leave them there for about one hour. Then we dig them up and they're nice and soft like potato and we eat them. No syrup or anything, just their natural taste. We give the little ones to the children because they've been following us all day and they're hungry. If anyone hasn't been able to go digging, we share *ganguri* with them too.

Women have lots of important roles, as natural farmers, as wives and as mothers. Women give out food to their children and husbands. There's always lots of food, *dhanpala* (mud mussels), *maypal*, shellfish, *ganguri* and vegetables. We also gather the wood and kindle the fires for cooking. This knowledge, women's knowledge, we want to share with other women. *Ŋapaki* women can come here and we can teach and share the Law of the women. If you're a girl, a baby, a teenager, a mother, a grandmother – you can learn with us, with our family.

Bawaka is important to women, it's female country. When tourists come, if they carry burdens, or sadness in their heart, they can start to heal, to feel healthy here. We do the same, children with problems from Yirrkala come here, Indigenous, non-Indigenous, we welcome them, they can feel free from their worries.

Ah, the clouds are drifting, rising over the water. At *djäpana* there are pinks and oranges, all telling us the story that this is harvest day. And the next story is about my favourite food. It's about the colour of the season, knowing which area to go to, knowing which sand is soft, and knowing how deep we need to dig.

While we wait for the *ganguri* to cook let me tell you the Burralku story. It's about how *ganguri* came to be here on the mainland. My grandmother, my mother's mother's clan, used to tell me this story. It's a sad one.

A story about *ganguri*

There was a man called Yuwululngurra – he was from the Galpu clan, and he and his clan were living on the coast, a group of them. He was a young man with two wives, and three children. He was very inquisitive, curious, always wanting to discover things.

One day he was walking along the beach after fishing and he saw a leaf, one single leaf floating on the waves. He stopped and picked it up and looked at it. He knew every leaf, every bark on the land but this one was very unusual. He wondered, 'Where has this one come from?' So he took it back to the leaders of the clan, the elders.

He showed them the leaf. They looked at it and they all

fell back. 'Where did you get this leaf from?' they asked.

'I found it floating on the *gapu*, on the waves.'

They were all thinking, 'Where is this leaf from – trees, shrubs, grass?', but no one had seen anything like that.

Yuwululngurra was lying down at night-time thinking and thinking about that leaf – maybe the leaf came from an island across the water. He thought, 'OK, tomorrow I will get into my canoe and paddle out there and see what I can find.'

Next morning he said to his two wives, 'Come on, bring the children, let's get in this boat and we'll go.'

The wives said, 'Where are we going? There is nothing out there.'

'No, we will find something, there is something, because that leaf floated over here and this current, this *gapu*, is coming out and coming in. It's only for a day and we'll go out there and see, and if we can't see any land we'll come back.'

So they got into the canoe and paddled out in the *gapu*, paddling and paddling and paddling until they couldn't see their own land. Finally they saw another land. 'There it is!' Yuwululngurra said, 'See, I told you, I told you this land is there,' and they kept paddling and paddling until they got to the little island at nightfall.

They slept there and the next morning when they woke up, Yuwululngurra said, 'Let's look for that leaf,' and they went looking all over the island, up over the rocks, finding only the usual plants and vegetation that you see on any island, but not that special leaf.

Yuwululngurra said, 'See, look! There's another island not far from here,' and the two wives said, 'You go, we'll stay over here with the children and get oysters, we will wait for you here.'

So Yuwululngurra jumped in the canoe and kept paddling to the next island. He paddled and paddled and could still see the island but night was falling. 'Gee,' he thought, 'I've paddled for quite a while, I can see both islands but I haven't got there yet,' so he slept in the boat.

When he awoke in the morning he could still see both islands, so he kept paddling. Suddenly the water looked like metal, like sparkling mercury. He picked up the water and it didn't get his hand wet, the liquid just flowed off his hand and his hand was still dry. 'What kind of water is this?' Yuwululngurra wondered.

He continued paddling and paddling, and saw that the island was getting closer and closer. He jumped out of the canoe and pulled it up onto the sand. Then he heard voices. There are people living here, thought Yuwululngurra, and he turned around to see a crowd of people saying, 'There's a new arrival.'

They came to grab him and Yuwululngurra thought, 'What kind of people are these?'

They felt his arms and they called out, 'He's got bones, he's got bones,' and he felt them and they had no bones, they were just flopping and flopping. He wondered, 'Is this Burralku? Yes, this must be the land of Burralku, the land of the spirits, the land of the dead.'

They said to him, 'We'll take you to the boss,' and they

dragged him to the boss. They checked his nose looking for the hole where they put the bone or stick through; they were checking to see if he had been through the Yinipi ceremony. He had a hole, this meant that he had followed the Law,

he was one of them. So they gave him fresh water to drink. They also gave him yams, oysters, fish, lots of everything. When he bit into the yam he said, 'What is this? This is so good, where does it come from?'

'Here, it comes from this place, Burralku,' they said.

Yuwululngurra asked, 'Can you show me the plant that this leaf belongs to?' And they showed him the leaves and the vines, *yarrata*.

'This is it, this is what I found floating on the water, so it comes from this place, Burralku,' said Yuwululngurra.

'But how did you find us? You're supposed to have no bones.'

'Because I was curious, I wanted to find this leaf to take back and show my people. I need to go back because I left my children and my wives on that island,' he said.

So they said to Yuwululngurra, 'You can go back to your family.' They gave him bags and bags full of yams and they gave him water and they did *bungul,* a dance, for him on the beach.

Yuwululngurra said goodbye and off he went. He paddled all the way back to his island. When he reached it he jumped off the boat, really excited. 'Hey, you two, I found it! It's *ganguri,* a beautiful big yam for us to eat.' He ran around the island looking for his wives, asking, 'Where are they? Where are they?'

Then he saw a shelter; in it were two adult skeletons and three skeletons from the children and their bags were just all hanging there with dust on them. Those beautiful bones, they had been there years and years and years. But Yuwululngurra was confused – after all, he had just gone to the island a day ago.

He broke all the bones, put them in his dillybag and paddled back home, wondering what happened, how could that happen? As he neared the shore he saw some children playing on the beach he only left a few days ago – and they said, 'All the elders, look! Look! Someone is paddling towards us.'

They were all standing there looking at Yuwululngurra. 'Who are you?' they asked.

'I'm Yuwululngurra.'

'No,' they said, 'who are you?'

He repeated, 'I'm Yuwululngurra, this is my country, I left here three days ago.'

'Come,' they said, 'we will take you to our elder.'

As they walked, Yuwululngurra was asking, 'Who are you people? I don't know you.'

Then the leader looked at him and said, 'You look like my brother's brother who got lost a long time ago.'

He said, 'I am Yuwululngurra, I am that brother but I left only days ago.'

They started arguing, the elder telling him that he'd left years and years and years ago.

So Yuwululngurra pulled out the *ganguri*, the yam he was given at Burralku, and he said, 'This is what I went looking for and here it is.'

They were confused. Eventually they decided that what was days for him was years and years for them.

So *ganguri* came to be on the mainland because Yuwululngurra went to Burralku to find it and that's why *ganguri* is sacred. Usually only the dead go to Burralku but Yuwululngurra is the man who went to Burralku alive and came back alive. He stayed on his land and always told that story to people. Some of the new people wouldn't believe him, but the old people did believe him because of the *ganguri* – there wasn't any of it growing on the land until he brought it back.

When my grandmothers
collected food, they saved it
in a basket and shared it. Now
we are putting our knowledge in the
basket and we share it – mother to
grandchildren – and now you have
to share it with your family.

LAKLAK BURARRWANGA

Laklak's Story 8

COMPUTER AND SPEAR:
MIXING KNOWLEDGES

In 2005, my family and I decided to start a business, Bawaka Cultural Enterprises (BCE). It is a tourism business, a business we have made to share our way of life with *ŋapaki*. It was part of my husband's dream that we live here and care for ourselves and our country. By being at Bawaka, starting a tourism business and writing this book, we are living that dream. We are able to take control of our own destinies. This is our dream. We are happy to share it with you. We hope that you will learn from it, learn from this book, and share what you have learnt with others.

Running the tourism business was my husband's dream. He was a smart man, thinking of the future for his children. We are the first Yolŋu people to start such a business. The business is about Bawaka people sharing knowledge with the world. This is the way of our future. The knowledge is from the land, we tell this to the tourists. They hear this and they cry and cry. In other places there's fighting – we're for unity and peace. We do it for the children.

We started getting the idea through Garma. Garma is a big Indigenous festival we have up here near Yirrkala every year. It includes ceremony (*bunggul*), song (*manikay*), art (*miny'tji*), dancing and workshops. When they first opened Garma, I thought it was just an open day with politicians, government people and other ŋapaki walking around. I used to hide, look and think, 'Who are these people?'

It was all the mums (remember, through *gurrutu*, all our mother's sisters are also our mums), who taught us. They not only taught us Yolŋu knowledge but, through Garma, how to link with Western knowledge and how to run a business. Now we run the cultural tourism program at Garma! We've met people from all over the world and shared our knowledge with them.

We have also started our own organisation, Lirrwi Yolngu Aboriginal Tourism Corporation, that brings all the Yolŋu tourism businesses together to support and promote tourism in East Arnhem Land. We called it *lirrwi*, the charcoal. Everywhere you dig in Australia you'll find some charcoal from the fires of Indigenous people. It shows that Indigenous people lived there, that we are from this place. There are layers and layers of it too, just like the *raŋan* and just like our knowledge. When you first dig, you'll see one layer of *lirrwi*; when you'll dig more, you'll see more. It's significant knowledge that goes down deep. It's from our ancestors. It's knowledge that's embedded in the land and that has been part of the lives of Aboriginal people for generations, forever.

For the future I see two worlds. I have been doing lots of book-writing, teaching, encouraging kids to go through college, starting the business. Lots of *ŋapaki* are coming and learning our knowledge, our Law. That is the bush university. I see the boy standing with the spear and I see the boy sitting on a rock at Bawaka playing with a computer. This kid can see a wider world, learning through a computer. That's the new generation, mixing the knowledges together. Then the boys can change over, boy with spear can play with computer and vice versa.

In this family, we live a balanced life. We value both languages, English and our own language. We talk both languages to our children. We speak both languages strongly. We believe in two-ways learning and in exchange. We believe in a future where we all learn from each other.

The government, though, it still tries to erase us. It cannot understand the two-way idea. Now there is a new Northern Territory government policy of erasing Indigenous languages from the school. We worked so hard to get a curriculum that builds on Yolŋu knowledge and ŋapaki knowledge. But the government is trying to take it out, to make our children foreigners in their own school even though we are the first people. We could learn from each other. Why can't the government see that?

The Intervention is like that too. The federal government imposed that onto us, herding us like cattle, just as the missionaries did, showing us no respect, ignoring our culture and trying to move us off our homelands. We tried to fight it, but now the government just renewed that legislation again. My sister Merrki (Dhalalu) was the face of that campaign and we all worked against it. But the government people didn't listen. They called it *Stronger Futures* but we don't see it that way. We see it as discriminating against our rights and treating us like second-class citizens. They try to bribe us, offering us homes and services that other people in Australia take for granted. But for us to get that, we have to give up culture, give up living on Country, be treated as if we have no strength, no knowledge, no Law.

Back in the 1960s, we fought for land rights and created the homelands movement so that our children could know Country and be strong in our culture. It was about us being in our home, having a right to belong where we are. We can be equal Australians. We can be Australians and have culture. We should have rights to be Yolŋu. For us, the homelands cannot be ignored. We can't run away from the kinship we have with Country and all the animals, plants, winds and spirits that dwell there. We have a place where we belong. That movement that we started forty-plus years ago, it still goes on.

We've got to stand on our two feet. Yolŋu should be in charge of the politics that affect us. It is time for a *yuta* (new) generation. Bäpa, he taught all the other Elders how *ŋapaki* work, their knowledge. And he taught Yolŋu knowledge to *ŋapaki*, so they could be equal. *Ŋapaki* politics and Yolŋu politics. *Ŋapaki* could see Yolŋu knowledge and Yolŋu could see *ŋapaki* knowledge. That is the most important thing, for young people of the future, to understand politics and *Rom* (Law).

Now I work with Sarah, Kate and Sandie – three university lecturers with beautiful hearts who come and write, using nice English. Every year they come here to help me with my family. I have written this book together with them and my family, for you, my readers. I want to let the world know about Indigenous people. I want us to share, to exchange. That's how Bawaka people are, sharing knowledge with the world, Indigenous and non-Indigenous. This is the way that our future will be.

I believe we need to tell the world about the first people of this Country. When you read this book, you will be able to go beyond what you hear on the television or from people who don't know. You can be one who learns two ways, who can balance the two worlds together. You can see that there are still Aboriginal people in the country who have a strong language, culture and life on Country. White men saw black men like a dream. They talked about the dreamtime. But Yolŋu weren't dreaming. We are not dreaming. These are our true stories that we have shared with you.

In the Yolŋu world, we have a library in the land. You can't destroy it. If you burn it, it grows again. This land is full of more knowledge than you can imagine.

djäpana

Djäpana, SUNSET

Endings

In the afternoon, all the ladies sit down on the beautiful white beach facing the sunset, while the kids are playing. The sun is going down and all the clouds are changing colour. It's called *djäpana*. So we are sitting and looking at the *djäpana* drifting around the sun. We are all feeling something inside our hearts. *Djäpana* makes the water really beautiful.

We hear the men playing *yidaki* (didgeridoo) and clapsticks while the sun goes down. *Djäpana* goes over the hills talking to the land. *Djäpana* is where the *walu*, the sun, ended up. We stay there looking at it and the kids are playing, twisting around in the white sand at Bawaka.

Every *djäpana* is the end of a story, the end of a time, for singing, crying, dancing. *Djäpana* is the last part. This is because *djäpana* is at the end of all our stories, all our songs, of the songlines. *Djäpana* is our Yirritja sunset. It is the sunset at Bawaka. It is also the end of our book. We have finished the writing, we have reached *djäpana*.

We have written this book for you, for all people, and for our granddaughters and grandsons. This book makes us strong because of the language, the land and the culture.

Naming all the language is very sacred in the Indigenous world. We have shared some of our language and some of our culture with you so that you can learn and you can share.

For Yolŋu, knowledge is told in context, at the right time and to the appropriate audience. If you are reading this, it is the right time for you to learn. You are told what you need to know and learn from this.

Djäpana brings a sorrow, the sadness you feel when you're leaving the land of Bawaka. You're leaving. We're sad. Our heart will always be at Bawaka.

Song for Djäpana

Rripa ngunha marrityi Warwu, Djäpana Galanggarri
Lithara biyma garrgarrnga wambalmirri dhatumirri
rrama djäpana.

[Colours of the sunset, names of the small clouds that gather around the sun.] Sometimes it makes us feel sad when we think about the people who have passed away.

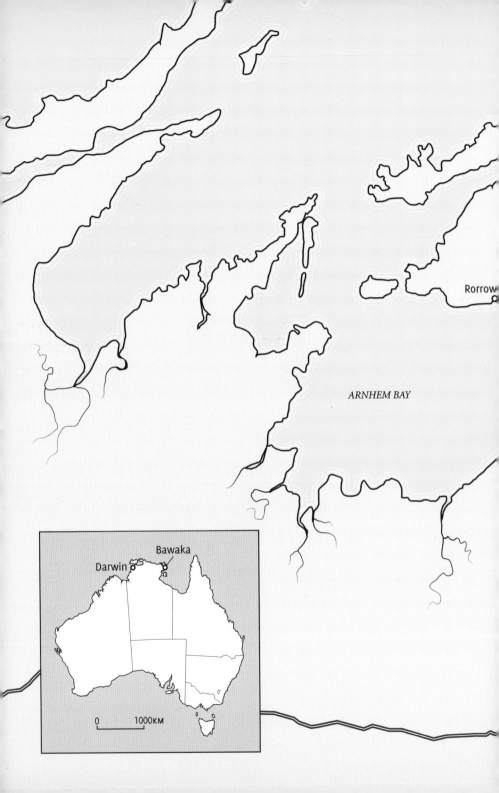

Rorrow

ARNHEM BAY

Bawaka

Darwin

0   1000KM

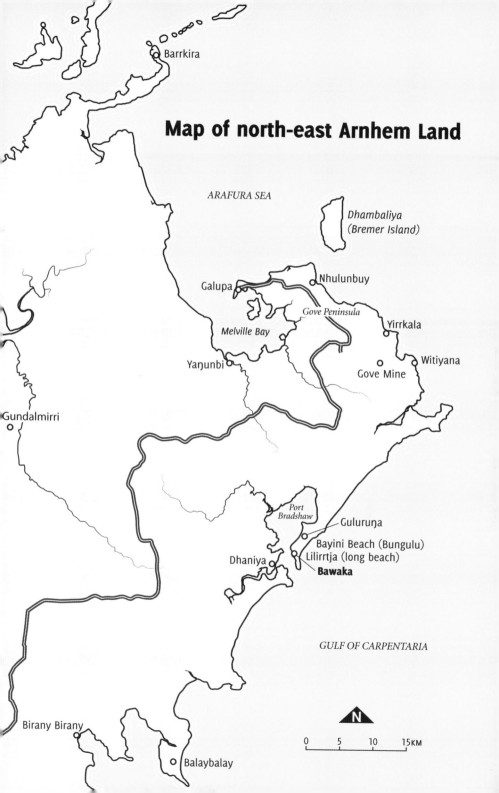

Map of north-east Arnhem Land

Barrkira

ARAFURA SEA

*Dhambaliya
(Bremer Island)*

Galupa   Nhulunbuy

Gove Peninsula

Melville Bay   Yirrkala

Yaŋunbi   Witiyana
                          Gove Mine

Gundalmirri

                                    *Port
                                    Bradshaw*   Guluruŋa

                                              Bayini Beach (Bungulu)
                          Dhaniya   Lilirrtja (long beach)
                                              Bawaka

GULF OF CARPENTARIA

Birany Birany

Balaybalay

N

0   5   10   15KM

Author note

Laklak and her sisters Ritjilili, Merrkiyawuy, Banbapuy,
and her daughter Djawundil, together with Sarah, Sandie and Kate,
are an Indigenous and non-Indigenous research collective. Academics
Sarah, Sandie and Kate describe the collaboration process.

Djawundil and Laklak   Kate, Sarah and Sandie   Dhalalu   Ritjilili (in front)   Banbapuy

The beach at Bawaka is at the heart of our research collaboration.
Laklak and Djawundil's house is on one side of the beach, and
when we stay at Bawaka we usually stay in Djawa's house on the
other side of the beach. The majority of our time has been under
the trees on one or other side of the beach. It is across this beach
that Laklak calls to let us know we should walk over to sit down
and talk. It is on this beach that Laklak and the other women of
the family sit down and share their knowledge with us. It is in the
sand of the beach that our children and grandchildren delight in
play. And it is across the beach that each day sees new layers of
footprints – dingo, crab, cane toad, seagull, crocodile, human –
tracking the interplay of knowledges and lives.

The group has worked as a research collective since 2006, and
jointly written two books and several academic and popular
articles. It was in 2008, at the launch of our first book (*Weaving
Lives Together at Bawaka*), that Laklak, her sisters and Djawundil

told us that they would like to keep writing with us; this book is the result. Many visitors come to Bawaka and they comment on how beautiful it is but Laklak and family want these non-Indigenous people to understand that Yolŋu people see far, far more; that underneath the beauty are many, many layers of knowledge, connections, obligations, communications and understandings.

Further reading

There is a wealth of amazing books and resources discussing the rich history and culture of north-east Arnhem Land. A few of them are listed here.

Burarrwanga L., Maymuru D., Ganambarr R., Ganambarr B., Wright S., Suchet-Pearson S. and Lloyd K., *Weaving Lives Together at Bawaka, North East Arnhem Land*. Centre for Urban and Regional Studies, University of Newcastle, Newcastle, Callaghan, 2008.

Dhimurru Land Management Aboriginal Corporation, *Yolŋu moṉuk gapu wäṉa sea country plan*. Dhimurru LMAC, Nhulunbuy, NT, 2006.

Hutcherson, G., *Gong-wapitka: women and art from Yirrkala, northeast Arnhem Land*. Aboriginal Studies Press, Canberra, 1998

In my father's country, videorecording, Tarpaulin Films, Mayfan Pty Ltd. Written and directed by Tom Murray and produced by Graeme Isaac, Australia, 2008.

Morphy, H., *Ancestral Connections: Art and an Aboriginal System of Knowledge*. University of Chicago, Chicago Press, 1991.

Saltwater: Yirrkala bark paintings of sea country. Australian National Maritime Museum, Sydney, 2003.

The Yirrkala Film Project, videorecording, Film Australia Lindfield, NSW. Writers Ian Dunlop, Philippa Deveson, producer Ian Dunlop, executive producer Chris Oliver, 1996 [2007 release].

Watson, H. with the Yolngu community at Yirrkala and Chambers, D. W. *Singing the land, signing the land*. Deakin University Press, Geelong, 1989.

West, M., *Yalangbara: art of the Djang'kawu /* produced in partnership with Banduk Marika and others. Charles Darwin University Press, Darwin, NT, 2008.

Williams, N. M., *The Yolŋu and their land: a system of land tenure and the fight for its recognition*. Australian Institute of Aboriginal Studies, Canberra, 1986.

See also the Bawaka Cultural Experiences and the Lirrwi Yolngu Tourism websites: http://bawaka.com.au and http://www.lirrwitourism.com.au

Thanks

We would first like to acknowledge Bawaka Country, which cares for us as we care for it. We are also indebted to our families – our mothers, grandmothers, partners, children and grandchildren – for their support in writing *Welcome to My Country*.

The research presented in this book was undertaken with financial and in-kind support from Macquarie University, the University of Newcastle, Lirrwi Yolŋu Tourism Aboriginal Corporation and Bawaka Cultural Experiences, and we are grateful to those organisations for their support. The results of part of this research project were presented at seminars at Macquarie University, the University of Newcastle and the Institute for Australian Geographers Conference in New Zealand, Cairns and Sydney; we thank the participants for their constructive feedback.

We thank Professor Michael Christie from Charles Darwin University for checking the Yolŋu text. We are extremely grateful to Dr Sophie Creighton (affiliated with the Australian National University) for her generous permission to reproduce and build on her recording and writing of Laklak and her sisters' life stories.

Thanks to Karen Young for her ongoing support and for introducing us to commissioning editor Sarah Brenan, to whom we are indebted for expert advice and guidance. Thanks also to Ruth Grüner for design and layout, and to Matt Grooby, Colin Majid, P J White, Melissa Kennedy and Rebecca Bilous, for their assistance with the text and images.

We thank Will Stubbs of the Yirrkala Art Centre for making artworks available (including the bark panels pages 73–4), and we thank individual artists for permission to use their work as follows: page vi, *Milky Way*, natural earth pigments on bark, by Naminapu Maymuru-White; page 9, *Macassan Boat*, collograph, by Laklak Ganambarr; page 19, *Mäna*, natural earth pigments on bark, by Laklak Burarrwanga; page 20, *Bäru*, screen print, by Gaymala Yunupiŋu; page 43, *Malpan*, linocut, by Dhalmula Burarrwanga; page 54, *Ganyu*, linocut, by Gulumbu Yunupiŋu; page 62, *Banumbirr Larrakitj*, earth pigment on hollowed pole, by Marrnyula Mununggurr; page 66, *Gan'yu*, linocut, by Dhalmula Burarrwanga; page 122, *Bäru*, screenprint, by Gaymala Yunupiŋu; page 138, *Macassan Boat*, etching, by Laklak Ganambarr; page 151, *Djirikitj*, screen print, by Gaymala Yunupiŋu; page 184, *Gunguri ga Wurrkadi*, etching, by Marrnyula Mumumggurr. The diagrams on pages 130 and 147 were redrawn by Guy Holt.

Yolŋu word list

We speak Yolŋu Matha, the language of the Yolŋu people. There are six extra letters in Yolŋu Matha that don't exist in English. One of them is the 'tail ŋ' (or soft 'ng' sound), used in *Yolŋu*, *raŋan* and many other words.

Special words for Gurrutu relationships are listed on page 206.

bakiki	wire
bamara	someone to be with
Bäpa	Father/Dad
bäpi	snakes
Bärra	rain that makes the sand soft (also the name of a wind) and a season
bäru	crocodile
bathi	basket
bawutj	king tides
Bäyini	the spirit women of Bawaka; also a people who visited north-east Arnhem Land long before the Macassans
bäyŋu	nothing
bäyŋu ŋalindi	'nothing moon'
bäyŋu walu	no sun (may mean wet season also)
bäythinyawuy	extra, left over
benydjurr	a sharp Dhuwa spear
betj	one sort of calm Yirritja water; see also mungulk
bewiya	rushes that stand in the rivers
borum	fruits
bukmak	everything, or everyone
buku-uŋgulmi	big mullet
buŋgawa	boss

buŋgul	ceremony, or dance
Burralku	land of the spirits, land of the dead
butjiriŋaniŋ	a type of bush medicine
dämbu miriw	four
Dätiwuy	Dhuwa clan group
dawu	fig tree (banyan)
dhalatpu	the green turtle
dhalimbu	giant clam, hard shell
dhaŋaŋ	many
dhan'pala	mud mussel
dharpa	wood, tree
dhäruk	language
dhimurru	a type of wind
dhum'thum	wallaby
dhuway	husband
dimbuka	dillybag
djäpana	the Yirritja sunset
djambatj	good hunter or spotter; also used for turtle hunter who holds the harpoon
djambatjŋu yirritjang	smart person, expert
djambaŋ	tamarind tree
djaykuŋ	filesnake
djilawurr	bush turkey
djinydjalma	crab. or mud crabs
djomala	casuarina tree

203

djin'pu	figs		*larrpan*	ceremonial spear cut from the mangrove
djunuŋguyaŋu	dugong		*lipalipa*	dugout canoe
djurrtja	small mullet		*lirra*	prongs on the end of the spear, teeth
duṯṯji	firesticks			
ga	and		*ḻirrwi*	charcoal
gaḏitjirri	grass spear used by kid		*ḻurrkun*	three, a few
galay	brother's wife		*ma'*	okay
galuku	coconut palm		*maḏwiya*	emu
gaḻpu	woomera or spear-thrower		*makarrata*	peace-making ceremony
ganguri	yam		*mala*	tribe (also means ten)
gänma	Yirritja place where waters mix		*mälk*	connection, skin names
gaṇṯal	catfish		*malwan*	a tree ofted used for spear-making
ganybu	spear used for freshwater fish		*manbuyŋa*	deep ocean water
gapu	water		*Maŋgatharra*	Macassan
gara	spear		*manikay*	ancestral song
garrtjambal	red kangaroo		*manutji ŋatha*	seeds
garrukal bird	kookaburra		*mapu*	eggs
gayit	shovel-nosed fighting spear		*maranhu*	foods
gaypaḻ	wattle		*maranydjalk*	stingray; rays and sharks generally
gonyil	meat, shellfish, eggs		*märi*	mother's mother and her brother
guku	honey, bee products, honey season		*marrawuluḻ*	calm water
guku gapu	honeywater		*märrma'*	two
gukuk	type of pigeon		*marrpaṉ*	large turtle
Gumatj	saltwater crocodile people		*matha ŋäṉarr*	tongue or language
gunga	pandanus, pandanus leaves for weaving		*mayawa'*	frill-necked lizard
gurrutu	Kinship		*maypal*	shellfish
gurtha	fire		*miny'tji*	art
guṯpa	type of tree used for spear-making		*miyapunu*	turtle
guya	fish		*miyapunu mapu*	turtle eggs
laḻu	parrotfish		*mokuy*	any sort of spirit
larrani	bush apple		*motj*	a cyclone
			muḏuthu	hawk-billed turtle

mukul	auntie
mukul bäpa	woman's mother-in-law
munbi	a vine vegetable
mungulk	rivers run rough coming into the calm water
murnyaŋ'	plant or vegetable food
mutitj	peaceful water
ṉämbarra	paperbark bush medicine (good for flu)
ṉamura	black-lipped oysters
ŋatha	root foods
naykuna	calm waters
nerrkada	cod
ŋalindi	the moon, month
ŋändi	mother
Ŋäpaki	non-Indigenous people, whitefellas
ŋaraka	bones
ŋatha	food; bush foods
ŋathiwalkur	a girl's grandmother's brother's wife's brother (avoidance relationship)
nhämunha'?	how many?
ŋulurr	the long rushes
ŋuykal	kingfish
räkay	waterlily bulbs
raŋan	paperbark
raŋi	low tide, beach
ritjilili	waves
Rom	Law
rrupiya	money
rulu	set, or pile of five eggs
ruwu	guts
waku	woman's son or daughter; or man's sister's children; or mother's mothers' mother

wäkun	mullet
walmuḏa	moon
walu	the sun; the day; time; sunshine
walupuy	daytime
wäŋa	homeland
waŋgany	one
waŋgany rulu	five
wapitja	digging stick
wapurarr	calm
warrakan	land animals and birds
wärrarra	Dhuwa sunset
wärrk	cyclone
wärrkarr	white lily (the white flower that indicates stingray season)
wäwa	brother
wetj	responsibility to share; counting and sharing
wilmurr'	everyday fishing spear
wirripikili	time of the new moon
wolma	lightning and thunder
wulu	a variety of sea grass
yambirrpa	Dhuwa fish trap made with rocks
yapa	sister
yidaki	didgeridoo
Yolŋu Matha	Yolŋu language
yothu-yindi	mother-child relationship – can also be between two men or between two pieces of land
yukuyuku	younger sibling
yuta	new

Gurrutu (kinship) system

Mukul AUNTIE
Ŋapipi UNCLE (mother's brother)
Mukul bäpa AUNTIE (father's sister)
Mukul rumuru POISON AUNTIE (mother's brother's wife)

Gäthu NIECE OR NEPHEW (brother's children)
Sister's children are your children (*waku*)

Märi GRANDMOTHER (mother's mother)
Momu GRANDMOTHER (father's mother)
Ŋäthi GRANDFATHER (mother's father)
Gutharra GRANDDAUGHTER OR GRANDSON (daughter's child)
Gaminyarr GRANDDAUGHTER OR GRANDSON (son's child)
Marratja GREAT-NEPHEW (brother's son's son)

Waku SON, DAUGHTER, CHILD
Dhuway HUSBAND
Galay BROTHER'S WIFE

Yapa SISTER
Wäwa BROTHER
Gutha LITTLE BROTHER
Miḏiku NAME A BROTHER CALLS HIS SISTER AS IT IS NOT
RESPECTFUL FOR HIM TO USE HER NAME DIRECTLY
Yukuyuku YOUNGEST BROTHER

Ŋamala and *Ŋänḏi* MOTHER
Bäpa and *Mälu* FATHER

Seasons

Dharraddharradya or Dhaarratharramirri
LATE APRIL, JULY/AUGUST
South-east or dry season; wind in east and south-east
Hunting for kangaroo, bandicoots, goanna.

Rarranhdharr
SEPTEMBER – OCTOBER
Hot, dry season
Fruits are ripening, stringybark and *wärrkarr* in flower.
Stingray and *miyapunu* season.

Worlmamirri
LATE OCTOBER – NOVEMBER
*The 'nose of the wet' or pre-wet season; thunder time,
maximum heat and humidity*
Good fishing and hunting for *miyapunu*.

Barra'mirri
LATE DECEMBER – FEBRUARY
Wet season, with heavy rains and thunderstorms
Plants grow and birds and animals are in abundance.

Mayaltha
FEBRUARY – MARCH
Rain falls less often, and the sun comes out to dry the land
Plants start to flower, and birds are everywhere.

Midawarr
LATE MARCH – APRIL
Harvest season (between the wet and the dry)
Bush foods become plentiful and fish numerous.

Index